The Other Casanova

Da Capo Press Music Reprint Series

GENERAL EDITOR

FREDERICK FREEDMAN

VASSAR COLLEGE

The Other Casanova

BY PAUL NETTL

𝄞 DA CAPO PRESS • NEW YORK • 1970

A Da Capo Press Reprint Edition

This Da Capo Press edition of
Paul Nettl's *The Other Casanova*
is an unabridged republication of the first edition
published in New York in 1950.

Library of Congress Catalog Card Number 73-107872

SBN 306-71896-0

Published by Da Capo Press
A Division of Plenum Publishing Corporation
227 West 17th Street, New York, N.Y. 10011

Manufactured in the United States of America

The Other Casanova

PLATE 1.

Casanova at Sixty-Three

PLATE 2.
Piazza San Marco by Francesco Guardi (1712-1793)

THE OTHER CASANOVA

A Contribution to Eighteenth - Century
Music and Manners

BY
PAUL NETTL

PHILOSOPHICAL LIBRARY
NEW YORK

PRINTED IN THE UNITED STATES OF AMERICA

To Wanda Landowska
in Old Friendship and Devotion

FOREWORD & ACKNOWLEDGMENT

This book is an attempt to view the history of music from the perspective of Casanova's "Memoirs." It will occasion no surprise among those familiar with the subject that in this endeavor Da Ponte, Casanova's kinsman in spirit, plays a major role.

Many readers know Casanova only as the dubious hero and raconteur of countless amorous adventures. Stefan Zweig, one of the keenest literary historians, put the case differently. "No chronicler of Casanova's period," he said, "and scarcely anyone who came after him—unless it be Balzac—ever invented so many situations or variations on a theme as Casanova himself actually lived through. No other life ever spanned a century in such a bold trajectory. It is no use turning up one's nose at his questionable prowess or to play the moralist on account of his illicit earthly career. . . . No, this Giacomo Casanova belongs to world literature, once and for all. He will survive his judges, endure when many writers of higher moral standards are forgotten."

In the rich and sumptuous life of this genial adventurer music, the theater, the ballet and the dance occupied a special place of their own. Historians of music and manners have made occasional use of Casanova's *Memoirs* as a source. But what is attempted here is to use the whole life of the man—not merely the *Memoirs*—as a source of musical history.

I owe sincere gratitude to Heinz and Ruth Norden, not only as gifted writers and translators, but also as friends. The English version of the book is their work and they have been most helpful in the design and preparation of the volume.

Grateful mention is also made of Mrs. Margaret Busch, Mr. Paul Müller, and Mrs. Frida Best. My warmest thanks go to Dr. Dagobert Runes, my understanding publisher.

The Italian paintings are reproduced with the permission of the firm of Alinari, Venice. The picture of Count Waldstein's Castle at Dux is reproduced by courtesy of Dr. Otto Gersuny, New York.

P. N.

CONTENTS

CONTENTS

LIST OF ILLUSTRATIONS

xi

CHAPTER ONE

CASANOVA, MAN OF THE THEATER

THE memoirs of Casanova are by far the most interesting and widely read of all eighteenth-century personal histories. Despite or perhaps because of their piquancy, they rank with the most important source material on the manners and morals of their time. It would be hard to find another figure of that age who saw, read, and observed as much as did Casanova; who was at home in all circles of the *haute* and *demi-monde;* who was on intimate terms with so many renowned and notorious men and women; and who told about everything he saw, heard, and did so absorbingly, with such unconcern, and with such superb humor.

Casanova was the son of an actor couple. The stage was in his blood. All his life he was on-stage—to the world and to himself. He was always out to hog the footlights, and when he had grown old he sat down to write his memoirs, again to steal the

I

show. He was an inveterate storyteller, braggart, and showman. Yet it was not braggadocio and self-conceit alone that induced him to write of his boudoir exploits. The old reprobate was a good deal of an exhibitionist. His prowess gone, he wanted at least to revel in his reminiscences. Hence his pell-mell concoction of truth and fantasy. The historian, nevertheless, can often lay bare the historical facts as though with a scalpel. Indeed, Casanova's piquant tales and background stories are bound to appeal strongly not only to the historian but to the theater lover, artist, and musician as well.

Casanova's aimless trips took him across virtually the whole of Europe. His last thirteen years were spent at Dux in Bohemia, as librarian to the Count of Waldstein, frustrated, jeered, almost a recluse. In that little German-Bohemian town he penned his memoirs, wrote innumerable letters, jotted down a thousand and one thoughts on scraps of paper, now preserved at Hirschberg, another little Bohemian town. A Dux manufacturer, a scholar by avocation, excerpted Casanova's many letters, writings, and notes. Whoever wished to delve into the life of Casanova, had to see his "major-domo," Bernard Marr, who was always ready to lend unselfish aid.

Casanova's memoirs, the original manuscript of which was always jealously guarded in the stout safe of the publishing house of Brockhaus in Leipzig are not available. Thus this most important original document can no longer be used. The scholar who seeks to explore the musical, cultural, and historical aspects of that life, must consult the so-called "Original Edition," or the complete German edition, edited by Conrad, if he would share the wizard's fortunes and adventures as a silent witness. He must also consult Casanova's other literary works, his correspondence and personal notes.

Gian Giacomo Casanova was born in Venice on April 2, 1725, the oldest son of an actor couple. Often during his lifetime he claimed to be of aristocratic origin. One of his ancestors, Don Juan Casanova, he said, had been Chief Steward to Pope Martin III. Actually, according to Gregorovius' *Lucrecia Borgia*, a certain Don Juan Casanova *was* Chief Stewart to Pope Alexander II. But that means little, since the name Casanova is almost as common in Italy as Smith is in England. At any rate, no noblemen have been discovered among Casanova's immediate ancestors. His grandfather was a shoemaker by the name of Geronimo Farusi, whose daughter, Casanova's mother, was named Gianetta (Zanetta in the Venetian speech). Since she came from Burano, she was nicknamed *La Buranella*, which calls to mind that the Italian opera composer Baldassare Galuppi, born on the same Venetian island, was dubbed *Il Buranello*.

Zanetta, our hero's mother, must have been a

3

beautiful and alluring woman. There can be little doubt that it was from her that Giacomo inherited his temperament. She was a fine actress who played a significant part in the history of the Italian theater. Even Goldoni devotes ample space to her in his memoirs. She began life as a respectable middle-class girl, presumably well sheltered by her parents, as was the custom in Venice. But then she met Gaetano Giuseppe Casanova, an actor from Parma. She married him in 1724—much against her parents' will—and gave birth to Giacomo the following year.

At the time Casanova was born his father was a member of an undistinguished company of strolling players. According to his son's testimony he was nevertheless a man of parts. His name seems to have left no trace in the annals of the Italian theater. He is merely known to have died at Venice in 1733, leaving Zanetta with three children in rather unsettled circumstances. Later on Francesco Casanova, the second son she had borne her husband, won fame as a painter of battle scenes. He was born on June 7, 1727 in London, where Zanetta was on the stage until 1728. There is an odd bit of intelligence, for which the Danish scholar F. J. Meier is authority, to the effect that King George II of England sired Francesco. Giacomo's second brother, Zanetta's third son, was Gianbattista Casanova, born on November 2, 1728, in Venice. He too became a painter, studying with **Rafael Mengs** and **Winkel-mann**, and ending up as director of the Dresden Art Academy in 1764. Casanova's third brother was an *abbé*, a dissolute fellow who never amounted to anything and of whom Giacomo's memoirs have nothing good to say. One of Zanetta's two daughters died in infancy while the other married Peter August, a teacher of the piano in Dresden.

By 1734 we find Zanetta back in Italy. She had attached herself to the well-known Imer company which played in the ancient arena at Verona.

Goldoni's memoirs reveal many interesting things about Imer as well as Zanetta. It would seem that Casanova's mother played a fairly significant role in the history of the *opera buffa*. Apparently Imer's company, of which Zanetta was the mainstay, brought the comic opera from Naples and Rome to Lombardy and the Venetian Province. To quote Goldoni:

"It was Imer's idea to introduce into the popular theater the musical intermezzo that was once regarded as the exclusive adjunct of grand opera, where it had to give way to the ballet. The comic opera originated in Naples and Rome, but was unknown in Lombardy and the Venetian Province. Hence Imer's idea fell on fertile ground. The innovation was entertaining—and very lucrative to the actors. One of them, Zanetta Casanova, a very attrac-

5

tive and gifted widow, played the leading ladies in comedy. Another had a wonderful voice but was quite evidently not an actress. She was Signora Amurat, who sang my serenade in Venice. Neither of these actresses nor Imer could read music but all three had musical taste, a good ear and an excellent stage technique.... Imer asked me to write an intermezzo for three voices and to finish it as fast as possible so as to have enough time left to have it set to music. Whereupon I wrote an intermezzo in three acts and called it *La Pupilla* [The Ward]. I based the plot of this little play on the director's own life, for I had noticed that he was very fond of the widow [Zanetta] and jealous of her. I had him play his real self. It did not take Imer long to discover this, but he thought the intermezzo so good, the satire so true to life, that he did not hold the jest against me. On the contrary, he expressed his thanks and congratulations and sent the work immediately to a composer in Venice whom he had previously interested in it."

Goldoni's intermezzo was set to music several times, by Galuppi, Paesiello, Ferdinand d'Antoine, and Salieri. I do not know who the first composer was. It is certain that Casanova's mother scored a great success in Goldoni's work; and since Pergolesi's *Serva Padrona* of 1733 is generally considered the first comic opera, Casanova's mother, appearing so successfully only a year later in an *opera buffa* by Goldoni, ought to be regarded as one of the god-mothers of this new opera type.

She did not stay long with Imer's troupe. In 1735 she went to Poland. Her youthful roles, however, did not endure very long. As long as she was young and beautiful, good fortune smiled on her, but with the fading of her charms her fame dwindled as well. Even in Poland she began to fall on evil days. She was subsequently engaged by the Elector August III (who was also King of Poland) as an actress by appointment to the Court of Dresden, and there she died. As late as 1761 Giacomo visited her in Prague whither she had fled with the Dresden Court when Frederic the Great besieged the Saxon capital in 1759 and 1760. By then Zanetta was in extremely straitened circumstances.

Goldoni set great store by Zanetta's acting talents. He deserves far greater credence than the Prince de Ligne who in his *Fragment on Casanova* described her acting as atrocious. One wonders whether Casanova may not have shared this view. On occasion he loved to be frank, sharp-tongued and self-contradictory. It is quite possible that he made derogatory comments about his own mother. This would have been quite in keeping with his character. The Prince de Ligne got his information from Casanova himself. We find, on the other hand, that the eighteenth-century author of a book called *Contributions to the History of the Theater* (Stuttgart, 1750) pays tribute to Zanetta's accomplishments.

Casanova's background shows where his adventurous streak originated. It is easy to understand why throughout his life he showed such an unquenchable passion for singers, dancers, and actresses. The graceful Zanetta had left an indelible impression on him. Perhaps it was his own mother he sought in all the actresses and ballet girls on whom he bestowed his love.

In early youth Giacomo was regarded as a dull-witted child. His mother paid scant attention to him. First she boarded him with an old woman in Venice, later she placed him with a Dr. Gozzi in Padua whom Casanova's memoirs describe as something of a half-wit. He nevertheless learned a great deal in Gozzi's home. It was there that he exchanged his first caresses with Bettina, his teacher's sister, in all likelihood receiving his first initiation into the secrets of the art of love. Quite apart from this, he made rapid strides during this period. He acquired a vast store of knowledge in classical literature. Because of his matchless memory he developed an uncanny capacity to sparkle with appropriate quotations on the slightest provocation. It was to this ability that he owed many a later conquest. When he left Gozzi's house, he took the first vows of the Church at Venice. But his accomplishment as a priest were at best dubious. No wonder! He was profoundly addicted to the luxury, glamour, and dissolution of the Lagoon City.

He had chanced into the social circle of Senator Malipiero, who at seventy-eight was still an epicure and liked to pick young actresses as his protégées. Among these Casanova encountered Teresa Imer, the daughter of the very stage director of whom Goldoni tells and who had engaged Casanova's mother as his leading lady. If old Imer had had a romantic liaison with Mme. Casanova, young Casanova now followed suit with the daughter. But Malipiero was jealous. One day he surprised the two in a compromising situation. Giacomo was caned and shown the door. The youthful *abbé* seems not to have been disconcerted. Casanova had already discovered Venice as the city of luxury, glamour, and immorality—the Paris of the eighteenth century. It was to Venice that Europe's profligates made pilgrimages to pay homage to famous courtesans, gamble in the *Ridotto,* seek mysterious adventures, participate in masquerades and processions—in short to taste all the charms of the city in the lagoon, its art, music, and festivities. At the same time Venice was the mecca of music and the theater.

CHAPTER TWO

LIFE IN VENICE

ANY book that seeks to do justice to the music
and theater of Casanova's time must necessarily take account of the theatrical and musical complexion of Venice in those years. Since olden times
the theater has been a favorite pastime of the Venetian—indeed, far more than a pastime, a feverish
passion. The Venetian himself is a born actor to this
day. His very presence, speech, and gesture are of
the theater. Stage improvisation, the *commedia
dell'arte,* had flourished for centuries, in Venice—
unrehearsed performances employing a handful of
well-known stock characters based on popular types.
Comedy was performed even in the streets. Make-
shift stages were set up on the docks and in open
squares and performances were given even in the
nooks and crannies of the Venetian ghetto. Heart
and soul of the Venetian theater was the "rhapso-
dy," an improvisation in which some talented nar-

rator, quite likely in rags and tatters, recited a dramatic incident. In 1786 Goethe witnessed such a performance and jotted down these lines:

> A tale I heard told, down there on the
>   well-paved embankments
> That hem in the City of Neptune, a city that
>   worships
> As though he were God the winged lion.
>   Densely the crowd
> Encircled the rhapsodist clad in tatter-
>   demalion.

Such storytellers and entertainers, often called *Filosofi* or *Cantastori,* together with their audience, were a picturesque sight in the squares of Venice. Their impromptu recitals depicted scenes from Greek and Roman mythology, and it was an inviolable tradition that the hero must die. This, in fact, led to the development of a specific "art of dying." Adherence to historical truth was not required. If Brutus and Caesar effected a swift reconciliation and Caesar was then struck down by the hand of Cleopatra, that did not matter. Frequently two characters were played by the same actor whose new disguise consisted merely of donning a wig in full sight of the audience. Karl Philipp Moritz, a writer friend of Goethe's in Rome, had made the acquaintance of a Venetian who had given up his original profession as a lawyer and subsequently toured the Italian cities as an impromptu player:

"When he is given a topic, he ponders for a few minutes and then begins to recite in a fixed rhythm. It is a real pity that some of these verses, uttered on the spur of inspiration, remain unrecorded by human hand, gone with the wind. This Venetian is an impromptu poet. He is of good family and held in great esteem and demand on account of his skill. His friends and his kin sought in every way to hold him to a regular way of life; but he repeatedly escaped them to follow his irresistible bent, roaming the cities of Italy as an improviser. He paid little heed to money. Such coins as he received, he flung about, by donning his filled hat and keeping only those for himself that chanced to lodge between his hat and his hair. At times this poet of the people was quite respectably dressed and powdered, with *chapeau bas* and sword by his side; at other times he went about in rags and tatters; for since he was in his own element in the unreal poetic world in which he dwelt, he paid scant heed to the common needs of life."

Usually some member of the audience, a lady, a scholar, or a nobleman, would set the topic. There was an interval in which the audience was entertained by the musician who was to accompany the impromptu minstrel. As a rule he was a lute or guitar player or a violinist. Meanwhile the player pondered his problem. Then the musician would strike up the tune to which the rhapsodist must chant his song. Ordinarily each meter had its own traditional melody. The *ottava rima* had a melody different from the *terzima rima,* the *"capitoli."* This was true as early as the fifteenth century, nor had it changed by the eighteenth. First came an invocation to a deity or Muse. Everyone listened with bated breath. No sooner had the first stanza met the approval of the audience when the mood was set.

The Venetians were never niggardly with admiration and praise. When the act had drawn to a close, the singer would rise. Wiping the sweat from his brow, he might engage in some banter with the audience while the musician struck up the tune for the second part, on a topic again set by a listener.

Such was the art of the Italian rhapsodist, a craft known but to the south and probably dating straight back to Homer. In 1725 the improviser Perfetti met with such acclaim in Rome that Pope Benedict XIII had him solemnly proclaimed poet laureate on the steps of the Capitol—an honor heretofore bestowed only on Petrarca. Napoleon himself was enchanted by an improvisation on the Battle of Austerlitz. So delighted was he that he granted the poet an annual stipend. Casanova, on his part, made the acquaintance of the famous impromptu actress Corilla to whom we shall revert later. As for Lorenzo da Ponte, he reports that in his youth he actually trained himself in the art of improvisation.

There were other types of comedians and entertainers that populated the alleys and squares of Venice at Casanova's time. There were puppeteers and magicians; fortunetellers on high platforms who whispered people's fortunes into their ears through long tin pipes; and the *Ciarlatano* who survives into our own day—the mountebank and quack, herb doctor, card sharp, and palmist who holds the destiny of his victims in the hollow of his hand.

All these entertainers were picturesque extras in the pageant of Venice. Demonstrators in American department stores who hawk their wares to musical accompaniment have ancient precedent, for the *Ciarlatano* also frequently softened up his customers with music. Such scenes were most common in the carnival season, in every teeming square, especially the *Piazza San Marco*, but also the *Riva dei Schiavoni*. Tiepolo painted many such scenes as did the Venetian genre painter Pietro Longhi.

There was a special aura to the theater of Venice at Casanova's time. There was, for example, Count Carlo Gozzi, the last noteworthy exponent of the *teatro dell'arte*, the impromptu comedy. There was no script for this type of play; it existed only in outline. The actors merely had to keep within the general limits of the plot. For the rest they improvised as they went along.

Before the curtain rose two copies of the scenario —the outline intended for the actors—were posted on the stage so that the comedians could inform themselves. But they had to recite their roles extemporaneously. Each performer had a mask and represented a certain type. There was *Pantalone,* the Venetian gaffer, a merchant with a black cloak and woolen cap, red camisole, close-fitting breeches, red stockings and slippers and a long beard. The *Dottore* was a lawyer, and since Bologna was the center of jurisprudence, he wore the traditional court and university garb associated with that city. His mask covered forehead and nose and usually he wore a nose fashioned of copper.

The most important actor, however, was *Arlecchino,* who together with *Brighella* formed the team called *Due Zanni.* The notion of these "two zanies" dates back to antiquity. *Brighella* was the cunning, mischievous servant in black livery and mask, a popular allusion to the sunburned complexion of the Bergamese. It is quite likely, however, that the black mask goes back to primitive concepts, to the demon of fertility who from time immemorial was pictured in black face—a dream character used to frighten children, identified by psychoanalysts with the image of the father slain by his sons. Instead of the term *Brighella* the names of *Finocchio* or *Scapin* were often used. *Arlecchino* was frequently called *Tracaguino, Truffaldino, Gradelino, Mezetino.* He too was always a servant from Bergamo but one who combined mischief with an air of stupidity. He spoke in an unmistakable dialect, and was dressed in rags and patches. On his head he wore a round hat adorned with a rabbit's tail, token of the Bergamese peasant, and whenever he appeared on the stage he whistled or sang or played the musical accompaniment, the *Bergamasca,* an old tune later familiar as a German song and used by Bach in the quodlibet of his Goldberg variations.

Of course *Zerbinetta,* the *Arlecchina* must not be overlooked; and there were many other stock characters of the *commedia dell'arte.* They used sundry dialects: the *Dottore* spoke Bolognese; the blustering, swaggering *Capitano Spaviento* used a jargon made up of Italian and Spanish, since he belonged to the Spanish occupation army. All these characters were somehow able to survive in opera. Even Figaro is nothing but a lineal descendent of the old *Arlecchino* and his Susan undoubtedly bears traits of *Zerbinetta,* just as *Dottore Bartolo* is, so to say, a grandson of *Dottore Graziano.*

Such was the stage setting with which Gozzi worked. Gozzi looked upon himself as the rediscoverer and champion of traditional impromptu comedy, and he waged bitter warfare against Goldoni who wanted to do away with these hoary trappings and ultimately succeeded. The literary battle between Gozzi and Goldoni and their disciples ended with the defeat of Gozzi and the old *commedia dell'- arte.* Goldoni became the reformer of the Italian comedy. Even though he used the old impromptu characters, he did away with facial masks as a monstrosity that made any facial expression impossible. He had raised the level of the old farce to one of true dramatic comedy, but he also posed completely new problems for the actors. He taught them to act with a freedom rooted in character and true-life observation. Yet he never repudiated his Venetian origin and the characters in his comedies are Venetian to the core. He showed up his fellow countrymen with all their good and their bad traits—the weaknesses and foibles of the upper classes, the fashion craze of the women, the dubious role of the *cicisbei,* those lovesick, disreputable youths who made a business of paying homage to the ladies of their heart from morning to midnight, often paid for their "services" by the ladies' husbands. He pilloried the gambling mania of the men who spent the nights betting in the *Ridotto,* while neglecting their wives. He pictured the manners and morals of the lower classes as well.

CHAPTER THREE

MUSIC IN VENICE

A S early as the sixteenth century Venice had
been the City of Music, and in the seventeenth
century it became the paradise of the opera. The
people of Venice are a happy breed compounded of
racial strains stemming from ancient Rome, the
Italian peninsula, the Slavic east and the Orient,
and they have an impressive musical endowment.
The Venetian loves color and pageantry. Even by
the year 1600 Giovanni Gabrieli had here brought
to life his pompous musical style, in which two or
more choirs competed in antiphony. We find this
antiphonous mode, undoubtedly going back to ancient musical practices of the Orient in the concertos of another Venetian, Vivaldi, as well.

The opera as an art form was created in Florence
and Mantua around 1600, but it was republican
Venice that freed the new art from the shackles that
had made it an exclusively aristocratic prerogative.
It was to Venice that the great Monteverdi moved

from Mantua in 1613, to take over the influential post of conductor of San Marco. Even earlier the art of the opera had been occasionally cultivated in such patrician mansions of Venice as those of the Mocenigo and Contarini. Interest in it had spread from here to wide circles of the citizenry, even leading to the establishment of a special opera house, the *Teatro San Cassiano*. It was at this time that modern, popular "show business" came into being. In Florence, Rome, and Mantua the opera had been a matter of the powers that be, of the most select aristocracy, who made the new art available only to themselves and their circle. But at Venice anyone who had the price of a two-lire ticket could go to marvel at the new sight. During the seventeenth century there were as many as four opera houses, generally playing at the same time. The commoners sat in the pit. The patricians rented the loges.

Even today, in the *Collezione Contariniana* (*Biblioteca Marciana*) at Venice, the visitor may leaf through the many librettos and scores of operas performed there in the seventeenth century. Prominent are the operas of Cavalli, Cesti, Legrenzi, Ziani, and Sartori, but there are many others. Many of these Venetians wrote infectious, swaying tunes in the manner of the barcarole, and some of them can scarcely be distinguished from the arias and chansons of operas of much later vintage.

In Casanova's time there were seven theaters in

Venice, each bearing the name of the patron saint in whose parish it lay. There was San Chrysostomo (the city's first theater, where Metastasio once had his plays staged), San Benedetto, San Samuele, San Luca, San Angelo, San Cassiano, and San Moise. Of these seven two usually served the *opera seria,* two the *opera buffa,* while three presented comedy. The season began in early October and ended with the carnival early the next year. There was a two-week recess during the Christmas season, but in return the *opera seria* again opened its doors for two weeks around Whitsuntide.

Except for Naples there was perhaps no other city in the world where the passion for music and the theater entered so deeply into the life of the people as in Venice. This applied especially to the "lower classes" who frequented the theater. The uproar was often so great that no one could be sure whether it meant applause or disapproval. The gondoliers were admitted free of charge whenever the seats in the pit were not sold out. During Goldoni's performances, however, the gondoliers were not entitled to seats by right but had to wait for their lords and masters in the street or in their gondolas. But Goldoni knew their value as a claque. He saw to it that they were accommodated in the corners of the theater.

Goldoni's comedy, *I Pettegollezzi* (Women's Gossip) deals with the life of Venetian mariners, and when it was first performed the uproar inside was so deafening that none outside the theater knew whether it was a hit or a failure. Handel's opera *Agrippina* was shown in Venice in 1709, to such scenes of enthusiasm that Handel's first biographer, Mainwaring, confessed himself unequal to describing them.

The patricians attended the theater masked so that they might bring their mistresses without hesitation and engage in certain "aristocratic" pastimes without let or hindrance. There was much laughing and roistering in the boxes and the "common herd" below were often peppered with lighted spills and other objects. A bald head spied below might very well attract a spitting contest. Apart from a number of aristocratic music fanatics who formed the backbone of the Venetian theater, most of the patricians indulged in these more or less harmless pleasures, the young men among them flirting quite openly with the chorus and ballet girls on the stage. The common people, on their part, took a passionate interest in all that went on on the stage. They were not content with applause. Verses and terms of endearment were addressed to the actresses, who would strut about dressed to the teeth, gesticulating, laughing, ogling the gentlemen in the boxes, conversing with the prompter, and all the while taking snuff.

About 1720 the composer Benedetto Marcello

published a satirical diatribe entitled *Il Teatro alla Moda* which attained great renown. In it he gave a dramatic picture of life at the Venice opera. The dress of theater patrons was prescribed by law. They were required to appear in *maschera e col bauttino al viso*. Ladies were permitted black gowns, but in that event they could not appear in the *platea*. The only freedom in dress was granted foreigners who made ample use of this license.

Marcello apparently did not hold Venetian theater audiences in high esteem.

"For the most part," he mocked, "the masked audience attends but the opera rehearsals, especially the dress rehearsals. They generally get into the actual performance by putting up only a small stake which they reclaim when they depart a quarter-hour later. In this fashion they get to see the whole opera in twelve nights [for nothing]. . . . Or they toady to the singers of both sexes in order to get inside the theater in their company without a ticket."

The illumination in the theater was poor, affording ample opportunity for gallant adventure. Two oil lamps flickered on wooden stands. There were neither chandelier nor lamps in the audience. A few lights were barely tolerated in the uppermost row of boxes, where two or three small individual boxes were often combined into a single larger one to accommodate a large and boisterous company. The poor musicians had to play by the light of a few

PLATE 3.
Nel Casotto dei Saltimbanchi by G. B. Tiepolo (1696-1770)

PLATE 4.

Il Ciarlatano by Pietro **Longhi** (1702-1762)

dim tapers. Whoever wished to follow the plot by the libretto had to bring along a candle and hold it in his hand. This meant that drops of wax were quite likely to fall on the book, which explains why so many Venetian texts preserved in the *Biblioteca Marciana* show traces of wax or tallow. The candles had an unpleasant odor, especially those used by the orchestra, a handicap that failed to deter the most fanatical patrons from making every effort to sit as close to the orchestra as possible. Such fanatics often had their servants preempt seats as long as an hour before the performance began. This in turn led to conflicts, not infrequently settled only by fisticuffs among the servants or duels among the masters. The hurly-burly in the theaters of Venice was unimaginable—applause, shouting, whistling, laughter, talk, noise, sneezing, coughing, yawning. Whenever a play by Goldoni was staged or one by his opponents Chiari and Gozzi, the whole audience took part in the show. There was wild enthusiasm and bitter controversy, and after the theater the discussion was continued at the Café Menegazza, the meeting place of the literati.

The admission price was collected by theater employees during the intermissions.* At the entrance

---

*Since the opening of the first opera house in 1637 the price of admission was set at four Venetian lire. In 1674 Francesco Santarini, impresario of the *Teatro San Moise*, reduced this to a quarter-ducat, which brought a general reduction. Only San Grosso Chrysostomo retained the old price.

doors crouched Venetian crones offering baked apples and pears for sale, which were consumed with a great smacking of lips during the arias or even the overture. Venders of anise water, pretzels, St. John's-bread, roast chestnuts, and almond milk shouldered their way through the audience. Coffee and ice cream were served in the boxes.

Again it is Benedetto Marcello who tells us of the shortcomings of the proffered refreshments under the aegis of the refreshment concessionaire. He was a music lover who always carried a scrap of music paper and served as the protector of all the artists. He supplied the entire theater personnel with drinks, at the same time dedicating to the primadonnas cantatas he had received from Naples. But "whether from sheer cunning or merely to play a joke on the innocent dupes the coffee he sells is adulterated with malt and beans. His buns are burned to a crisp. His different liquors, each with its own name, are all brewed from the same common brandy and honey. Some of the beverages seem compounded of sulphuric acid and dried-up lemons, with salpeter or ashes in place of salt. . . . Wine and food brings four times its value."

There were as yet no playbills at this time. Two signs giving the name of the play were posted on the Rialto and the Piazetta, and these were the only public announcements of the night's program.

What were the operas that flourished in the time

of Casanova? Casanova often mentions *Il Buranello*, a name that refers to Baldassare Galuppi, born 1706 on the island of Burano. After many years spent abroad *Il Buranello* died on January 3, 1785 at Venice. He was one of the most distinguished composers of comic operas and between the years of 1722 and 1773 no less than fifty-one different operas of his were performed at Venice, quite apart from many staged in other cities of Europe. He lived in London and later St. Petersburg and was the first foreigner to write Russian church music. From 1748 on he supplied Venice with operas regularly.

Another Venetian opera composer of this age was Galuppi's teacher, Antonio Lotti (1667-1740), organist and later conductor at San Marco. He too lived abroad for some time, becoming a pillar of cultural life at the court of Saxony. He composed no less than seventeen operas for Venetian consumption. Another figure of importance was Antonio Vivaldi (1680-1743), a priest dubbed "*il preto rosso,*" on account of his red hair. He was also a violin virtuoso at the church of San Marco and head of the girls' conservatory *Ospedale della pietà*. Vivaldi too wrote many operas, but his real strength lay in instrumental music to which he gave a style that bears his name to this day. Significantly enough, he staged at San Marco and the conservatory concerts so colorful and magnificent that even Johann Sebastian Bach was inspired to adapt them for the harpsichord and perform them. Only against the rich background of Venice could this art form have arisen and flourished.

Song runs in the very blood of the Venetian, is as important as life itself. When Burney, famed British historian of music, undertook his "musical journey," he was particularly fascinated by the musical life of the people of Venice. "The people here," he said in *The present State of Music in France* (1771), "at this season seem to begin to live only at midnight. Then the canals are crowded with gondolas and St. Mark's square with company; the banks too over the canals are all peopled, and harmony prevails in every part. If two of the common people walk together arm in arm, they seem to converse in song; if there is company on the water, in a gondola, it is the same; a mere melody unaccompanied with a second part is not to be heard in this city; all the ballads in the streets are sung in duo. Luckily for me, this night a barge, in which there was an excellent band of music, consisting of violins, flutes, horns, basses, and a kettledrum with a pretty good tenor voice was on the great canal and stopped very near the house where I lodged; it was a piece of gallantry, at the expense of an inamorato in order to serenade his mistress."

Goldoni says in his memoirs: "There is singing in the streets and on the canals. The merchants sing as they hawk their wares. The workmen sing when going home from work. The gondoliers sing while awaiting a fare."

When Goethe visited Italy in 1786, he was especially drawn by the mariners' songs of Venice which impressed him deeply. At the time the heroic and romantic songs of Ariosto and Tasso were still being chanted to ancient, fixed tunes. Yet this art was dying out even at Goethe's time, and the great poet had much trouble finding two gondoliers who were still skilled in the old airs. At Casanova's time this traditional popular art still flourished.

Goethe stepped into his gondola by bright moonlight, placing one of the singers forward, the other aft. One of them then struck up the tune, to be spelled by the other when one stanza had been sung, and so on in turn. They sang every stanza to the same basic tune, but with melodic variations in harmony with the shadings in the text. This "ancient mariners' style" seemed a trifle crude and noisy to Goethe, and he and his companion went ashore, leaving one of the gondoliers in the gondola, while the other moved off about a hundred paces. Now Goethe listened to these hoary songs in the fashion in which they were commonly heard in Venice, and the master was content.

"The silent canals," he said, "the tall buildings, the soft moonlight, the deep shadows, the spectral aspect of the few gondolas that glided to and fro—all this enhanced the singular character of the scene, nor was it easy amid all these circumstances to perceive the nature of this exquisite chant. It perfectly befits the idle, lonely boatman, lying stretched out at ease in his craft on the canal, waiting for his master or for a fare—this spinning of fancies from boredom, fitting poems known by heart to this song.

"Sometimes the gondolier raises his voice as loudly as possible. It sounds far across the quiet surface. All else is quiet. And in the midst of a great, populous city the singer seems to be almost alone in his solitude. Another still gondola drifts past him, the ripple of the oar scarcely to be heard. Far off someone hears the song—in all likelihood an utter stranger. Thus poem and tune unite two men who do not know one another. One becomes the other's echo, and he too now seeks to be heard. Tradition requires the two to alternate stanza by stanza. The song may last for many nights in this fashion and the two converse without ever tiring. The listener who passes between them partakes of their singing, while they are preoccupied with themselves. From a distance this song sounds inexpressibly poignant, for only with a feeling of distance does it find fulfillment. It sounds like a dirge without mourning, yet it inevitably brings tears to the eyes. My companion, otherwise not a particularly sensitive man, said: '*E singolare, come quel canto intenerisce, e molto più, quando lo cantano meglio.*'"

Goethe goes on to relate that the women of Lido,

especially those from the outermost villages, Mala-
mocca and Palestrina, likewise sang the verses of
Tasso to these and similar tunes. "They are in the
habit of sitting down by the shore, when their men-
folk have put to sea to fish, and to intone these
chants vigorously until they hear the echo of their
dear ones sounding in the distance. How much more
haunting is the beauty of this song here than when
a lonely man sounds it so that a far-off stranger of
like mind may answer! Here it is an expression of
the heart's keen yearning, at any moment close to
the joy of gratification."

Rousseau, in his *Dictionnaire de Musique* (1768),
likewise tells of the barcaroles sung in Venice to the
poetry of Tasso. In 1743 and 1744 he had been secretary to the French embassy at Venice. As we shall
see, Casanova came to Venice in the spring of 1744,
while Rousseau left his post in the fall of the same
year. Thus the "Citizen of Geneva" and our adventurous hero breathed the air of the City of the Lagoon at the same time. Could it be that they met?

The palace of the French embassy, a building in
the baroque style, lay in the San Geremia quarter,
not far from the old ghetto, near the *Ponte San
Giobbe* which spans the *Canale Canareggio*. The
apartment of Secretary Rousseau was on the third
floor. Down below in the canal his gondola was
moored. He had a first-row seat in all the theaters.
The Republic of Venice was zealous in seeing to it

that every foreign diplomat was plentifully supplied with theater tickets, and their distribution
was the concern of the "Eminent College of Foreign
Affairs." Rousseau visited this agency on behalf of
the French legation, and for the fall season of 1743
as well as for the carnival and Whitsuntide season
of 1744, he was given boxes at San Chrysostomo,
San Angelo, San Salvatore, and San Samuele. Rousseau himself became an outstanding opera addict.
As he tells in his *Confessions,* he had brought with
him from Paris the prejudice against Italian music
frequently found in France. "I soon come to love it
with the passion it inspires in everyone who is capable of judging it."

Rousseau's musical impressions at Venice were of
far-reaching importance not only to him as a philosopher of music, but to the whole history of music
in France. Even more than by opera, however, he
was entranced by Venetian folksongs. "Made for the
people," he wrote in his *Dictionnaire de Musique,*
"and set to music by the gondoliers themselves, they
are so rich in melody, so pleasing in accent, that
there is no musician in all Italy who is not eager to
learn and sing them. The free admission to the theater which the gondoliers enjoy enables them to
train ear and taste without cost. They compose and
sing their own tunes as men who take all the finer
points of music into account, yet prefer the simple
and natural manner of the barcarole. The text of

these songs, like the common speech of those who sing them, is usually more than robust. But whoever delights in true portrayals of the people and is fond of Venetian speech to boot will be quite carried away by the beauty of the melodies, and many connoisseurs have made great collections of them."

Rousseau was perhaps the first to call the attention of the rest of the world to these ancient Venetian folk tunes, and it is quite likely that it was only through him that Goethe first took note of this interesting phenomenon. Thus the profound impression he carried away of the Tasso recitation of the Venetian gondoliers may be owing to the philosopher of Geneva, whose own songs in *Les Consolations des Misères de ma Vie* were published after his death in 1781. In this work we are made acquainted with a *Psalmodie nouvelle sur le Tasse* and a *Tasso alla Veneziana*. The *Psalmodie* is a kind of aria recitation to the text *Canto l'armi pietose,* while *Tasso alla Veneziana* is a melismatic piece reminding in its musical embellishments of Spanish folksong. In this connection mention should be made of a certain *Canzoni da battello,* gondolier songs found in an eighteenth-century manuscript in Venice. These Venetian songs clearly show the mutual influence that existed between opera and folksong.

CHAPTER FOUR

CASANOVA THE FIDDLER

THE Venice environment in which Casanova grew up was steeped in music. Yet his memoirs are silent on what impressions, if any, he received while watching his mother act and sing in Imer's company—in which, by the way, Goldoni also had an interest. Unless we are utterly mistaken, these boyhood impressions were so powerful as to shape his whole adventurous career.

Italy was the land of comedy and song, and in this sense Venice was its capital. The young *abbé* was a frequent guest in the house of Giuletta, a singer whose later career at the Vienna opera was brusquely interrupted only by the Chastity Commission of Empress Maria Theresa. At that time Giacomo was fascinated by Giuletta, but she cared little for him and treated him coldly because he failed to do full justice to her charms. Casanova had thousands of adventures of this kind and indeed, the famous catalogue aria by Da Ponte and Mozart, in which

Leporello sings about his lord and master Don Giovanni, fitted him perfectly:

> Now among them were countesses,
> Servant-girls and citizens,
> Princesses and marchionesses,
> There were ladies of every station,
> Every form and every age.
>
> With the blondes it is his custom
> To command their gentle manners,
> With the brunettes, constancy,
> With the fair ones, their sweet ways.
> He wants plump ones in December
> But in June they must be slender,
> While the tall ones must be stately
> And the small one must be sprightely.
> Old ones, too, he has not missed,
> Just to have them on his list;
> But his favorite form of sinning
> Is with one who's just beginning.
> Whether they be rich or poor,
> Fair or ugly—one thing's sure:
> Just provided they are women.
> You know well what happens then!

Casanova began his career as an adventurer in Venice, his home town. He arrived there on April 2, 1744, after a brief journey through Italy which he made after taking his vows. But his *wanderlust* soon drove him on to the Orient. (Gugitz found discrepancies and contradictions in Casanova's description of this part of his life.) He exchanged his clerical garb for a uniform and after various adventures arrived at Constantinople in mid-July 1744. There he spent a happy interval, nearly becoming a Moslem and marrying a harem girl. But Turkey could not hold him long. On the way home he fell in with evil company at Corfu and lost all his possessions. He arrived at Venice in December 1745, poor as a church mouse.

What, then, does an actor's offspring do when he is down on his uppers? He takes to the fiddle. From his old teacher Dr. Gozzi Casanova had learned just enough to get by in a theatrical orchestra. The San Samuele orchestra accepted him and he earned a dollar a day. San Samuele was the theater built by Giovanni Grimani in 1655, but operas were given there only from 1710 on. Casanova was second violinist until April 15, 1746, during a season in which the operas *Il Pandolfo* by Giuseppe Scolari and *L'Olympiade* by Ignazio Fiorillo were performed among others.

Giacomo had been engaged by the theater through the intervention of one Grimani, his friend and sponsor. Grimani was a member of the patrician family that had built the theater in 1655 and who still owned it. Casanova's mother had frequently played comedy roles there.

As was unavoidable, Casanova slipped a few not-

34

ches in the social scale as a result of his new employ-
ment. As an orchestra musician he could not show
his face in high society. This was characteristic of
his whole life. Whenever he appeared in the guise
of an adventurer or mountebank, he at once gained
entry to the best circles of society. But when he was
a professional musician—the most decent profession
he ever practiced in his life—"respectable society"
slammed the door in his face. His new profession
did bring him adventure, nevertheless—romantic
promenades along the waterfront and in side alleys,
and the opportunity to play the violin at parties,
weddings, and banquets. It was a lighthearted, merry time. After the theater was over, there was the
inevitable visit to the tavern, where one would im-
bibe a few glasses too many, and later on the night
was spent in questionable company. . . .

This, then, was Casanova the musician. He did
not last very long at this profession. It was not
merely that he had become "socially inferior." In
all likelihood he simply did not take to music as a
profession in this form.

CHAPTER FIVE

HENRIETTE, THE CELLO PLAYER

IN 1749, on a trip to Parma, Casanova had an interesting encounter. He met a charming girl whose name he gives only as Henriette and about whom little else is known. She turned out to be an accomplished musician. When Casanova finally came to recognize and admire her musical talent and her mastery as a cellist she said to him: "If you hadn't happened to tell me a month ago that you have no taste for music, I would certainly have told you that I am a very good cellist; but I know you: if I had said so, you would have hastened to get me an instrument, and your friend does not wish to entertain herself with something that bores you."

Casanova also mentions elsewhere that he cared little for music. After a visit to the *Teatro via Pergola* in Florence in 1761 he said: " I took a box next to the orchestra, to eye the artists rather than to hear the music of which I was never an enthusiastic admirer." Yet there are other passages in which he professes to be a great music lover. And the Casanova archives hold notes that disclose a considerable grasp of music.

But to get back to the charming, cello-playing Henriette. Casanova loved her tenderly. She was one of the great passions of his life and, understandably enough, he fulfilled her every wish. Since she was a great admirer of music, he took her to the theater in Parma, to see an *opera buffa* with music by *Il Buranello*. As mentioned earlier, Buranello was Baldassare Galuppi, and there is reason to believe that the opera which Casanova attended with his beloved was *Arcadia in Brenta,* very popular at the time. The Library of Congress in Washington has two copies of the libretto, dating from the year 1750. Another Galuppi opera, *Il Protettore della Moda,* was also performed frequently in 1749. Whichever it was, Henriette probably enjoyed Galuppi's music thoroughly and Casanova undoubtedly got his money's worth. . . . The finale of the second act was so good that Casanova had to get his friend the score. She must have busily followed the music with its help and we can almost see her gallant escort lighting one or two candles for her so that she could read the better as he gazed into her beautiful eyes.

A mutual friend invited the couple to a private recital at his country home near Parma. Henriette was long hesitant to accept the invitation but finally yielded. And a charming musical interlude ensued which Casanova remembered all his life.

It was one of those distinguished house concerts in the rich tradition of eighteenth-century culture. So that Henriette's social charm might stand out all the more, no other ladies had been invited. Soon the artists arrived. Chief among them was the famous Laschi, described by one source (Oehler, *Geschichte des gesamten Theaterwesens in Wien*, 1803.) as a "fine and sensitive *buffo*, an excellent singer, sincere and expressive in his presentation." With him was a Signorina Baglioni, described as "very pretty at the time." She was descended from a great family of singers that later boasted the five Baglioni sisters (Vincenza, Clementina, Giovanna, Costanza, and Rosa). Burney, Laborde, and other music historians mention them. Burney heard them in Florence, Milan, and Vienna in the years 1770 to 1772, and since he writes that they were then quite young, Casanova's Baglioni may well have been their mother. The famous tenor Antonio Baglioni, who created the first Ottavio in Mozart's *Don Giovanni* at Prague in 1787 was another member of this family.

The program at the concert included a symphony, played by an orchestra, whereupon "the two singers sang a duet, displaying much taste and great talent." Following this, a pupil of the great cellist Vandini played a concerto. Presumably it was one written by Vandini himself, and if the soloist approximated his teacher's performance, it must have been an inspiration to listen to him. Burney had met Antonio Vandini at Padua in 1770 and called him one of the greatest cellists in the world. "The Italians applied the word *parlare* to his playing, meaning that it was as expressive as the human voice." Vandini played in the Church of San Antonio in Padua, but he also toured Europe. In 1723 he went to Prague together with the great violinist Tartini to attend the coronation of Charles VI. He stayed on for three years at the home of Count Kinsky. He, Nardini, and Padre Martini were Tartini's favorite pupils. A close and almost sacred friendship of fifty years' standing bound Tartini and Vandini together. According to Minos Dounias, *Die Violinkonzerte Giuseppe Tartinis,* Dissertation, 1935, Tartini wrote a number of beautiful cello concertos for his friend.

In any event the concerto by Vandini which his pupil played, enchanted Henriette to the point where she abandoned all reserve. She seized the musican's cello and asked the orchestra to begin the concerto over again. Casanova had had no inkling that the girl—one of the many victims of his passing fancy—was such a great artist. He trembled like a leaf as soon as she began to play. When the beauty and volume of her playing rose above the orchestra, his excitement mounted to fever pitch. The storm of applause made not the least impression on Henriette. Without raising her eyes from the score she played six more movements and when she had finished she turned to the musician and said apologetically that she had never played on a better instrument. Casanova was so moved by this incident that he went out into the garden to "shed a thousand tears of love and emotion" over this lovely creature.

Later on he suggested that Henriette give concerts, and I am quite tempted to believe that he would have liked to exploit her artistic gifts to his own advantage. What is really significant, however, is that Casanova emphasizes how Henriette, whom he bought a fine instrument, turned him into a passionate lover of music which hitherto, as he often stressed, had not meant a great deal to him. "One might claim, I believe, that a man who is averse to music is bound to become its ardent admirer if the performer to whom he listens is a past master and is adored by him." Indeed, even Casanova's enthusiasm for music has an erotic coloration. If Tolstoi in his *Kreutzer Sonata* treats of the theme in terms of "From Music to Passion," Casanova's life goes "From Passion to Music."

CHAPTER SIX

THE PARIS OPERA

A S we have seen, Casanova occasionally liked to picture himself as contemptuous of music. But his memoirs as well as the notes jotted down in his old age show a remarkably acute judgment in all musical matters. Indeed, not a few of his notes become valuable source material for the history of music.

In 1750 he saw Campra's *Fêtes Venetiennes* in the Paris Opera. The theme naturally interested him as a Venetian, and he was highly critical of the stage sets. "An excellent orchestra began playing an overture—very good in its way. Then the curtain rose and I saw a handsome stage set, purporting to represent the *Piazza San Marco,* as seen from the isle of San Giorgio; but to my dismay I saw the Palace of the Doges to my left and the great Campanile to my right! Precisely the reverse of reality. I could not help laughing at this inexcusable blunder. True, the music was good, although somewhat old-fashioned, but it entertained me only at the beginning and then only because it was new to me; later on it began to bore me. The monotony of the lyrics and the noisy shouting that broke out in the wrong places soon tired me. These French lyrics were supposed to be an improvement over the Greek mode and our own recitative, which the French find repulsive. Well, they would love it if only they understood our language."

For forty years, ever since 1710, Campra's *Fêtes Venetiennes* had been part of the Paris Opera's repertoire. The classic French style of this opera was indeed antiquated. The more modern Rameau was then in fashion, and German as well as Italian music had taken hold of the French imagination. It was in 1750, as a matter of fact, that the lively new symphonies of the Czech composer Johann Stamitz had been introduced in Paris. They were enthusiastically received by the mercurial French. No wonder Casanova found Campra's music old-fashioned and dry despite its charming instrumental interludes. He was, moreover, inured to Italian music, to the operas of Galuppi, Scarlatti, and Pergolesi.

The relative merits of French and Italian opera were the topic of keen debate in the Paris salons of the time. The controversy even goes back to the seventeenth century. In Lully's *Ballet de la Raillerie* French and Italian music appear as allegorical characters, each praising its own virtues. In his instrumental work *Concentus Musico Instrumentalis* (1701), the famous German composer Johann Josef Fux, too, used two melodies—a kind of *Aria Italiana* and an *Air Françoise* thus pointing up the esthetic contrast between the two styles. One year later, in 1702, *Abbé* Raguenet wrote his *Parallèle des Italiens et des Français en ce qui regarde la Musique et les Opéras*, championing the Italian ideal in music. He was opposed by the Frenchman Lecerf de la Vieville who, in 1704, dismissed all the innovations of Italian music, which he called contrived and piquant, by saying that they went beyond the limits set by nature.

It is quite evident that even those Frenchmen who came into direct contact with Italian music, such as Montesquieu, were forcibly reminded that their otherwise fickle countrymen were rather conservative in their musical taste. They had failed altogether to shake off the influence of Lully and it was the Italians who were blazing new trails in music. Small wonder, for French rationalism did not stop short of music. The true Frenchmen paid more attention to the proper emphasis of words than to a beautiful melody. Thus the contrast between French and Italian music can be reduced to two words: rationalism versus emotionalism. Yet it remains a curious paradox that the high priest of rationalism, Jean Jacques Rousseau, would have none of it in music, while Rameau, the great French composer, in his *Traité de l'Harmonie* of 1722, set as his rationalist goal the recapture of what he called lost music values. Rousseau, in his *Lettre sur la Musique Française* (1753), delivered a devastating blow to the decaying edifice of French baroque opera.

"The ear," said Rousseau, "will no longer tolerate the scholarly nonsense of your fugues and double fugues, inverted canons and *bassi obligati*." The German-born encyclopedist, Baron Melchior von Grimm, in his pamphlet *Lettre sur Omphale,* used the same line of argument in defending Italian music, at a time when all Paris was split into two bitterly hostile camps, the "Buffonists" and the "anti-Buffonists." We shall see later what this same Baron Grimm had to say about French music in his pamphlet, *Le petit Prophète de Boehmisch-Broda.*

It so happens that we have further independent confirmation of Casanova's musical observations in Paris. Sara Goudar, later one of Casanova's paramours (she was one of the many women he "almost" married) wrote in her memoirs: "The spontaneously cheerful French yawned at the opera in Naples, and the Italians never failed to sleep soundly at the opera in Paris. I recall how a Venetian who, toward the end of a performance of *Les Fêtes Venetiennes,* asked a Frenchman in the adjoining box: 'Pardon me sir, but when will they begin to sing?'

44

'But counfound it, sir,' the Frenchman answered almost in tears, 'they have been singing for some four hours!' 'Forgive my question,' the Venetian replied, 'but at home we call that declamation, not song.' "

I feel certain that the Venetian whom Sara Goudar mentions, was Casanova, who so disliked the monotonous style of French singing with its unmotivated shrieks. French opera knows neither the richly-rounded arias of the Italians nor their rapid-fire recitative delivery. It was precisely this melodramatic singsong style, neither aria nor recitative, slavishly following the text and constantly changing pace and rhythm, which Casanova, the full-blooded Italian, could least stomach. He shared this prejudice with Goldoni, who wrote in his memoirs (1787) that he found French instrumental harmony impressive and precise, though the overture as a whole left him cold. It was during the overture that the Italian had to sit through the fugues he considered so tiresome and arid. Patiently he waited for the arias to begin. Came the ballet—a sign that the act was drawing to a close—and still no aria! So he made his provocative inquiry of his neighbor.

Yet no less than six arias had been sung in the various scenes! And Goldoni had thought of them all as recitatives! . . . Casanova's own memoirs show that the Paris public reacted quite differently. He describes an incident when he went to hear a Lully opera in the company of his friend, the Venetian

Ambassador de Marosini. "I sat in the orchestra," Casanova wrote, "just below the box of Mme. Pompadour whom I did not know. In the first scene the singer Le Maux made her entrance and uttered such an unexpected shriek that I thought she had gone mad. I guffawed in all innocence, not thinking that anyone would take umbrage. But a blue-beribboned gentleman who sat next to the Marquise asked me brusquely what country I came from. 'Venice,' I replied in the same tone of voice. 'I was there,' the gentleman rejoined, 'and I too laughed very much—at the recitatives in your operas.' 'I believe you,' Casanova replied, 'and I am sure that no one tried to keep you from laughing.' It turned out afterward that it was none less than Richelieu who had been so scornful of the Italian recitative.

Georg Keyssler, the very scholarly tutor to Baron Andreas Gottlieb von Bernstorf, who in turn was Prime Minister to the Elector of Brunswick-Luneberg, published a book entitled *Recent Journeys Through Germany, Bohemia, Hungary, Switzerland, Italy and Lorraine* (second edition in 1751). These journeys had been undertaken some twenty years earlier and in 1730 Keyssler had visited Venice.

"Among the finest diversions of the Carnival and Whitsuntide season," he wrote, "is the Italian opera, on which I deferred reporting to my master until I should have heard the Venetian version. There can be no doubt that the Italians surpass all other nations on this score, and it is unpardonable presumption for the French to compare their own opera to that of Italy. True, the stage settings in Paris are fine, and the dancing and ballets in the intermissions excellent. Then too, the French make their recitatives more palatable by having them follow the style of arias, and they make more use of the chorus and the duet than do the Italians. These are matters in which the Italians might well learn a lesson or two. But as for the music and the staging, the French are far behind. Their arias are usually arranged as *chansons à boire,* with so little variation as to be almost monotonous. The singers stretch out the *semitonia* or *transitiones* from one note to the next, usually emphasizing them by a trill or a tremolo on the last syllable.

"French audiences don't like an opera unless they are able to hum the arias the next day. It is a different matter with the arias on the Italian opera stage. The people have a natural talent and love for music, but it takes some time before they learn to sing the artful arias of their opera stars. Even skilled voices never learn some of the Farinelli and Faustina numbers. Possibly the Italians grant their vocalists too much freedom to display their craftsmanship. Perhaps the ideal opera would be one in which the Italian and French styles were fused.

47

"So far as instrumental music is concerned, Paris is above reproach, boasting really excellent musicians. Guignon, an Italian has no peer on the violin. Demarets and Battiste shine with the viola da gamba, Blavet with the flute, Fabio with the archlute."

As for Casanova, it is clear that scenery and ballet were far more important to him then the music, and in these respects it was the French opera that was far ahead of its Italian counterpart. Casanova had a friend in Paris, the attorney Claude Pierre Patu, himself the author of a play, *Les Adieux du Goût,* woven around the operatic controversy of 1754. Patu could hardly wait to take the Venetian to the opera, and Casanova was eager to go, because the scene of the opera happened to be Venice. He criticized almost everything and it must be admitted that he had a keen eye. Let us hear what he said about the performance:

"The plot unfolded on Mardi gras, with the Venetians promenading over the *Piazza San Marco* in masks. The stage teemed with gallants, procuresses, women engaged in romantic intrigue. The costumes were odd and out of character, though as a whole the opera was entertaining.

"I had to laugh at one incident that appeared rather absurd to a Venetian. From the wings emerged the Doge and the twelve members of the Council, all dressed in quaint long robes and cavort-

ing about. Next came a tall, handsome, masked
dancer, with an immense black wig that tumbled
halfway down his back. His robe reached to his heels
and was open in front.

" 'That's the inimitable Duprès,' Patu said to
me, admiration in his voice. I had heard of Duprès
and paid careful attention. The impressive figure
advanced with measured steps. Reaching the front
of the stage, the dancer slowly and gracefully raised
and moved his arms, now stretching them out, now
crossing them, all the while executing some nimble
and precise footwork, leaps and pirouettes. Then
he vanished like the wind. The whole interlude
took scarcely half a minute. Applause and bravos
sounded from every corner of the house. I was
amazed and questioned my friend.

" 'Why, the applause is in tribute to the grace-
fulness of our Duprès, the divine harmony of his
movements. He is sixty years old, but those who
saw him forty years ago swear he is unchanged.'

" 'Do you mean to say he always danced like this?'

" 'Well, he could not have danced better. What
you have seen was perfection, and what could go
beyond that?'

" 'Nothing—unless perfection is only relative.'

" 'Here it is absolute. Duprès does the same thing
over and over, yet each time one thinks one sees it
for the first time. Such is the power of true beauty

and nobility. This is the very essence of the dance and of harmony, something of which you Italians know nothing.'

"At the end of the second act Duprès again put in his appearance, his face masked as before. He danced to a different tune, but to my way of looking did exactly the same thing. He stepped close to the footlights and stood for a moment in a gesture of perfect grace. Patu insisted that I must admire him, and I admitted that I did.

"Suddenly I heard a hundred voices calling from the pit: 'Good God, good God, watch him grow, watch him grow!' It did seem as though Duprès' whole body were elastic, as though it were unfolding and growing in size. I made Patu happy by telling him that Duprès was indeed the essence of grace.

"Immediately afterward a ballerina raced across the stage like a fury, making *entrechats* to the right and left and in every direction, though she never leaped to any considerable height. She was nevertheless applauded with something approaching frenzy.

" 'That's the famous Camargo,' Patu told me. 'I congratulate you, my friend, for having reached Paris in time to see her, for she too is past sixty.'

"I admitted that the dance had been most impressive.

" 'She was the first dancer on our stage,' my friend

continued, 'who dared make leaps. No woman did so before her. The most remarkable thing is that she wears no drawers.'

" 'Pardon me, I saw . . .'

" 'What did you see? That was her skin. True, it isn't made of lilies and roses.'

" 'I don't like Camargo,' I said, my voice contrite. 'I prefer Duprès.'

"An old admirer who stood to my left told me that in her youth Camargo had executed the Basque leap and even the *gargouillade* without ever exposing her thighs, though she danced barelegged.

" 'If you never saw her thighs, how do you know she wasn't wearing tights?'

" 'Ah, there are ways of finding out such things. I see the gentleman is a stranger here.' "

In Campra's opera Casanova had occasion to see the greatest contemporary dancers. Duprès was the founder of the art of expressive dancing, the teacher of Noverre and Vestri. He was the classic exponent of the baroque ballet. A choreographer as well as a dancer, he created his own dances. As early as 1722 he set Paris afire, and his grace and marvelous presence continued to delight Parisian audiences when he was past sixty. He was dubbed *Le Grand,* which referred not merely to his great height, for he also earned other nicknames—*Le Dieu de la Danse, Apollon de la Danse.* His specialties were the *cha-*

connes and *passacaglias* by Campra and Rameau, which he danced in mask.

As Duprès was the greatest dancer of his time, so was Maria Anna Cuppi Camargo (1710-1770) the greatest ballerina of Paris. She was Spanish—the first in the great line of Spanish dancers—and the niece of a Spanish Inquisitor. "Perhaps," Grimm once ironically remarked, "the pleasure she gave thousands with her *entrechats* made up for the sins of her uncle." Despite her many affairs, she is supposed to have been as unhappy offstage as she appeared happy behind the footlights. At least her contemporaries thought so. She was the first to dare to execute leaps on the stage and this meant throwing the traditional heels and long skirts into the discard. Camargo was the inventor of the short ballet skirt (*tutu*).

Paris connoisseurs divided their loyalties between Camargo and her rival, Mlle. Sallé. Sallé was an exponent of the "expressive dance," Camargo of toe dancing. Sallé wore the classic *tunique,* Camargo the *tutu.* Perhaps it was this that gained Camargo the support of male Paris in her youth, and the matter of the drawers may not have been unimportant. Even Baron Grimm, the encyclopedist already cited, dicusses the subject in his *Correspondence littéraire*:

"Mlle. Camargo, sister of the violinst Cupis and known in theatrical circles for her countless gallant adventures, acquired immortality in the theater by introducing the leap. It was she who first dared to have her drawers shortened, and this useful invention, which enabled the amateur to appraise the dancer's legs knowingly, was later universally adopted.

"At the time, however, it threatened to cause a very dangerous split in opinion. The Jansenists decried the scandalous heresy and would not tolerate the shortened drawers. The Molinists, on the other hand, insisted that the innovation recalled the spirit of the primitive church, that it was intolerable to see *pirouettes* and *gargouillades* impeded by long skirts. The pillars of the opera strove long to resolve the disciplinary point in the sacred doctrine which threatened to divide their followers into two camps.

"In the end inspiration descended on them and they found a way out of the predicament which suited everyone. They decided in favor of shortened drawers but ordained at the same time that henceforth no dancer must appear on the stage *without* drawers. This edict has since become a cardinal point in the orthodox church, having been universally accepted by the powers behind the scenes as well as by the faithful who frequent the sacred places."

According to the *Souvenirs de la M. de Crequi* (IV, 58) Camargo was also the first one to wear shoes without high heels. Even Keyssler had admired her at Paris. Reporting on the Italian ballet to his master, Keyssler wrote: "These ballets cannot be compared to the dancing at the Paris Opera, any more than Camargo, now in Paris, has her peer in the ballet."

What chiefly impressed Casanova at the Paris Opera was the lightning speed with which the sets were whisked away and replaced. This, he remarked, was altogether unknown in Italy. He also admired the quiet behavior of the audience, something that must have seemed most unusual to an Italian. On this subject he wrote: "In Italy one grows rightly irked at the noise that prevails while the artists sing. It cannot be overemphasized how absurd is the silence that instantly follows this bedlam when the dancers appear. . . ."

But let us examine the Campra opera Casanova heard. It was a sequence of five episodes, having in common only the fact that the scene was always Venice. The first scene, *Les Serenades et les Joueurs,* has a plot composed of intrigue, mistaken identity and masquerade, distantly reminding of themes from *The Marriage of Figaro.* Two girls, Irene and Lucile, love the same youth, Leander, and ultimately join forces against him. Leander arrives with a troupe of musicians to serenade Irene. In the darkness Lucile takes Irene's place, and the scene ends in general confusion. The second scene, *Le Bal,* is

PLATE 5.

Il Ridotto by Pietro Longhi (1702-1762)

PLATE 6.

Il Ridotto by Francesco Guardi (1712-1793)

interesting in musical respect. A dancing master and a musician get into a quarrel about the merits of their respective arts. The musician demonstrates the composition of a piece depicting a storm at sea. The wind whistles. Sleep, Spring, the nightingale enter into the work. The conclusion is formed by a Venetian *furlana*. In the remaining scenes, *Les Devins de la Place Saint Marc, L'Amour Saltimbanque,* and *L'Opera,* programmatic instrumental music likewise plays an important part. The various scenes of Campra's opera, by the way, could be combined in different fashion. Casanova witnessed, in addition to the prologue, *Les Devins, L'Amour Saltimbanque* and *Le Bal.* He criticized the costumes as being out of character, and also the beat of the conductor "who struck out to the left and right with furious motions, as though he could set the instruments going by the mere power of his arms. I detested him."

Perhaps it may be as well to take a momentary glance at the history of the conductor's art. There was, in the eighteenth century, a sharp contrast between the Italian school of conducting while seated at the harpsichord and the French style of beating out the rhythm. Italians, Germans, and even Frenchmen inveighed against this latter style, introduced by Lully, which ultimately prevailed throughout Europe.

The French manner was rooted in the growth of

55

complex instrumentation, the frequent change of time, and the precision sought by the French orchestras. (Even Casanova admired this precision. "I found the way in which the orchestra started as though with a single stroke of the bow delightful," he wrote.) Yet Rousseau said: "How the ears are assailed at the Paris Opera by the unpleasant and unceasing noise caused by the conductor with his baton! ... The Paris Opera is the only theater in Europe where the rythm is beaten out and not followed. Everywhere else it is followed without being beaten out."

Baron Melchior Grimm, in his *Le Petit Prophète de Boehmisch-Broda,* described the French conductor as a *bûcheron* (wood chopper). Among the Germans, Quantz (Marpurg, *Historisch-Kritische Beiträge,* 1754-62, I.S., 238) and J. F. A. Hiller (*Anweisung zum musikalisch richtigen Gesange,* 1774, V. 8) criticized French conducting. Mattheson in his *Exemplarische Organistenprobe* (1719) and *Grosse Generalbass-Schule* (1731), was especially sharp: "It is a curious thing that our fellow countrymen never seek to learn from the French their propensity for hard work and precision, their firmness in the keys, their unison in playing and their other good qualities. Instead we Germans seem to be attracted only by their arm-waving and their sawing of the air, the weird contortions of hand and foot, body and soul, which they employ in their conducting. In this we strive mightily to ape them, even taking pride in the fact."

Yet one does the French wrong in attributing to them alone responsibility for the noisy misuse of the conductor's baton. A hundred years before Casanova, in 1649, Daniel Friderici had reproached foolish conductors for "laying about with the baton that the chips fly"; and in 1687 another German, Daniel Speer, had complained that during performances the thunderous beat of the conductor could be heard farther away than the singers. True, Germany never witnessed an incident such as the death of a conductor from the consequences of an injury suffered from his baton, as happened to Lully in 1687. *Bûcheron* actually became the barbed nickname of one French opera conductor. The method of conducting *à la Bûcheron* soon invaded Italy from France and ultimately spread to other parts of Europe. Only a few years after his sojourn in Paris, Casanova undoubtedly encountered this style in his homeland.

On October 3, 1786, in the conservatory of the *Mendicanti* Church at Venice, Goethe attended the performance of an oratorio. He voiced his displeasure at the French style of beating out the time in these words: "It would have been most enjoyable, had not the accursed conductor knocked out the time with a roll of music against a grille, with such brazenness as though he were dealing with schoolboys. . . . I know that the French have it that way. I had not thought the Italians capable of it, yet the public seemed used to it."

CHAPTER SEVEN

BALLET MUSIC

THE Library of the Paris Conservatory possesses a copy of the 1731 edition of Campra's opera with magnificent engravings. A Venetian landscape theme is added as a vignette to the *Prologue du Ballet des Amours de Venus,* which together with, or in place of, *Le Triomphe de la Folie sur la Raison dans le Temps du Carnaval,* served as a curtain raiser. The illustration supports Casanova's judgment that the Paris opera lacked realism. But when Casanova calls Campra's music tedious, it is in order to put forward a strong defense against such a charge. The opera remained on the program until 1759—Grimm discusses it in his *Correspondence littéraire*—and this alone shows its popularity. It is a really excellent revue, with dances, explosive instrumental effects, fair women, and fine landscape scenes. The ballet music is certain to have been impressive.

Many of the ballet and instrumental pieces must have stuck in the mind of the one-time theater fiddler—*passepieds, espagnoles,* the great *chaconne* with chorus at the end of *Saltimbanque,* built on the *basso ostinato* familiar from the Venetian school of the opera, the overture that came in the middle of *L'Opéra,* the *bourrées,* the *Air des Menuettes,* the *Air des Bisgayens,* the *quadrilles,* the different *Airs des Masques, des Arlecchins, Polcinelles,* etc. Then there was an Italian *da capo* aria in *Le Bal,* which was meant to parody the Italian coloratura style.

These and many other things should have drawn Casanova's notice, had he paid attention to the music rather than to other things during the performance. . . .

But before taking leave of French opera, let us once more give the floor to Baron Melchior Grimm and his fascinating pamphlet, *Le petit Prophète de Boehmisch-Broda.* Grimm here sought to ridicule old-fashioned French opera, as against the Italian *opera buffa* on the one hand, and the Bohemian and German symphonic school of Mannheim with its verve, energy, and heretofore unknown melodies. Founder and chief exponent of this Mannheim school was Johann Stamitz, born in *Deutschbrod* in Bohemia, who had just scored a great success in Paris. We can scarcely reproach Baron Grimm for his little geographic slip, which made him confuse *Deutschbrod* with *Boehmisch-Broda*.

His "Little Prophet of Boehmisch-Broda" came to Prague as a young student, eagerly to pursue his studies in an attic in the *Judengasse* and to fiddle at barn dances and weddings. In mysterious fashion he was suddenly translated to Paris, hurled in the midst of the opera. He was appalled at its "unnaturalness" against which he held up his simple and artless Bohemian minstrelsy. Let us hear what he had to say about Paris conductors:

"As I was thus soliloquizing (for I love to talk to myself when I have the time), I noted that the orchestra had already begun to play, though I had not even noticed it. They played something they called an overture. I saw a man with a stick in his hand and I thought he meant to chastise the many poor violins I heard among the few good ones. He made a noise as though he were splitting wood, and I was only surprised that he did not dislocate his shoulder. The power of his arms amazed me. I thought about it (for I like to ponder when I have the time), and then I told myself: 'Oh, how often is talent misplaced in this world, and yet genius manages to reveal itself, even when it is not in its proper place! If this man,' I said to myself, 'were born in the house of my father, which stands only a quarter-mile from the forest of Boehmisch-Broda in Bohemia, he might be earning up to thirty pence a day. His family would be rich and respected, his children would roll in luxury. And people would say: "Look at the wood chopper of Boehmisch-Broda—there he goes!" And even if his skill were not so great, it would still suffice to earn him his bread and the wine he drinks in the tavern.' And I noted that what he did was called 'to beat out the time.' Yet though he beat it strongly, the musicians were never together. And I grew sad when I thought of the serenades we Jesuit students were in the habit of singing in the streets of Prague at nightfall. For we always sang together, even though we had no stick.

"And then I saw a man who did even better, and they shouted *'la chaconne, la chaconne!'* But he said nothing and I admired him as he showed his body, his arms and his legs from all sides, for he was handsome, and when he turned about he was still handsome. And his name was Duprès. And I saw a shepherd come with his shepherdess, and found them to be masked musicians, for I saw clearly how they wrote on the floor the arias that were being played, tracing out with their footsteps each eighthnote. And the rhythm was precise and I admired their dance, for I know my way about music. And their name was Lany. And I saw men and women dancers without number and this was called a festival, though it was really not, for there was no joy, and there seemed to be no end to it. I found that these people never grew tired of leaping about, though their faces had a bored expression, and they bored me and the others. And their dances constantly confused the actors, and just when the actors were about to speak their parts, the ballerinas came and the actors were herded into a corner to make room, for them, though the festival was designed only for the actors. That was the way the author had written it. And when the actors had something to say, they were permitted to come to the center, but when they had spoken their piece they were sent back to their corner. And I found that we did these things better. For our actors have nothing to do with the dancers. They have always finished their part when the dancers appear. Well, I am only saying what I am thinking.

"It seemed to me that the author should get very angry at the dancers for interrupting the conversation of his characters for no good reason. And I concluded that he must be a kindhearted man, for he allowed his actors to call the dancers, even though they had no business on the stage. Indeed, he even went so far as to say that the dancers must be present, though I still believe they had no business to be there. And in this fashion I was bored for two-and-a half hours, while listening to a collection of minuets and arias, called *gavottes,* and other dances they give the names of *rigodons, tambourins* and *contredanses.* The whole was intermingled with

63

a few scenes of Gregorian chant, such as is sung with us down to this day at vespers, and with a few songs I had already heard in the suburbs of Prague, especially in the White Cross Inn and the Archduke Joseph Inn. And I saw that in France this is called an opera and I made notes to aid my memory."

At Paris Casanova came to know virtually all the famous actresses and opera singers. He had met the gracious and gallant Balletti, a dancer and later an actor, at Milan as a young man, and the two had made the journey to Paris together. Balletti now introduced Casanova to the home of his mother, the famous actress Sylvia Balletti. Sylvia was one of the greatest artists of her time, the mainstay of the *Théâtre Italien* in Paris. Frederic the Great, who speaks of her as *"La Sylvia, aujour la meilleure Actrice du Royaume,"* had vainly offered her an engagement in Berlin.

Casanova soon came and went in the Balletti home as though he were a member of the family, and for a long time he regarded himself as officially betrothed to Sylvia's daughter Manon. It was at Sylvia's house that he came to know all the theatrical celebrities of Paris. Often it was his first friend Patu who introduced him to noteworthy people, and these particular theatrical acquaintances cast a highly significant light on the manners and morals of Paris society at the time of Louis XV.

Casanova, for example, grew acquainted with the famous singer Le Fel, to whose house Patu had invited him. She was the primadonna of the opera, and both Campra and Rameau created many parts expressly for her. Naturally she was a celebrated member of the Royal Academy of Music. During his first visit Casanova noted three charming children of tender age cavorting about. He put on an ingenuous air but did admit that he was struck by the fact that none of the children resembled another.

"I should think so," the primadonna commented. "The eldest is the son of the Duke d'Annecy, the second of Count Egmont, and the youngest was sired by Maison-Rogue who has just married La Romainville!" "But I thought," Casanova retorted in some perplexity, "that you were the mother of these charming children!" The assembled company burst into laughter. Casanova still had a good deal to learn in Paris, before becoming the great arbiter of the art of love.

Casanova's tale, by the way, is in conflict with Rousseau's account of Le Fel in his *Confessions*. Grimm, it appears, was desperately in love with the singer, but she would have none of him, since she was at the time enamored of the author and philosopher Lenis de Cahusac. Grimm spent whole days in deathly lethargy, and it was only owing to the efforts of Rousseau and Raynal that he was ultimately rescued from his agonies.

On another occasion Patu took Casanova to see Lany, ballet master at the opera. Here his experiences were not unlike those at the house of Le Fel. He met a few thirteen and fourteen-year-old girls, whom he treated to pleasantries that were received with demurely cast-down eyes. One of the young ladies complained of a headache, adding that she thought she might be pregnant. Casanova, in some surprise, remarked that he had not believed Madame was married. Again the company burst into laughter and Casanova was once more stamped as the "innocent country bumpkin."

CHAPTER EIGHT

DRESDEN

In mid-August 1752 Casanova traveled from Paris to Dresden where, as we have seen, his mother was actress by appointment to the Royal Court of Saxony. While he was still in Paris, the Polish Count von Looz had persuaded him to translate Cahusac-Rameau's *Zoroastre* into Italian, and on January 17, 1752, the opera was performed at Dresden, together with Metastasio-Hasse's *Adriano in Siria.* This is what Casanova tells of his work:

"I was to adapt the words to the choral music, a difficult task. The music did indeed retain its virtues, but there was no sparkle to the Italian verses!"

As it happened, only the overture and a few choral pieces by Rameau had been retained for the Dresden performance of *Zoroastre.* The remaining music had been contributed by Johann Adam, Royal Ballet Composer—proof of the low esteem in which Rameau's fine music was held. Casanova's libretto was preceded by a *Protesta*—an apology for the fact that the opera theme was not in harmony

67

with Christian dogma. The purpose, it was stated, was merely to present a revue composed of various ballets, show pieces and novel instrumental effects.

In Dresden Casanova met his mother, and in her honor he wrote a tragicomedy built around harlequin characters. "It was a parody of Racine's rival brothers. The King laughed heartily at the witty barbs with which my piece was studded, and I received a splendid present from his hand. . . ." (It amounted to 200 dollars, half of which was paid in February, the remainder in March 1753).

But more about *Zoroastre*. The title page of the libretto is reproduced, and the playbill read as follows:

Zoroastro, Institutore dei Maghi	Bernardo Vulcani
Amelita, Erede pretendente del Trono di Battro	Marta Bastona-Focher
Abramano, Primo Sacerdote degl'Idoli	Gioachino Limperger
Erinice, Principessa di Battro	Giovanna Casanova
Zopiro, uno delli Sacerdoti degl'Idoli	Cesare Darbes
Zelisa, Giovane Battriana	Isabella Vulcani
Cefia, Giovane Battriana	Paola Falchi-Noe
Abenide, Giovane Seluaggio Indiano	G. B. Toscani
Cenide, Giovana Seluaggia Indiana	Isabella Toscani
La Salamandra	Paola Falchi-Noe
Un Silfo	G. B. Toscani
La Vendetta	Pietro Moretti
Una voce che sorte dalla Nuvola infiammata	il Signor Focher
Altra voce sotteranea	

Battriani e Battriane, Saluaggi Indiani, Maghi, Popoli Elementari, Sacerdoti degl'Idoli. Demoni e seguito della Vendetta. Le Gelosia. La Collera. La Disperazione. Le Furie. Pastori. Ninfe.

A so-called "comedy bill" for the opera is preserved at the Saxon State Library, in a collection embracing the years from 1749-1754, and thus I am able to reproduce its content:

"Zoroaster—A Tragedy

"Performed at the Royal Theatre in Dresden during the carnival season in the year 1752.

"*Summary*:

"In the first act the wickedness of the godless Abramano is revealed. He seeks to ascend the throne of Bactria, vacant on account of the death of the last king, young Ferres. By means of intrigue without number he seeks to exclude from the throne Amelita, a Princess of the blood royal, for she refuses to accept his love, instead favoring his enemy Zoroaster. Abramano insinuates himself into the favor of Erinice, another Bactrian Princess, who is seduced by her ambition for the empire Abramano offers her, though she too has some affection for Zoroaster. Thus she comes to share in Abramano's evil doings. He initiates her into his magic powers and by their means she gains hold of Amelita.

"In the second act Zoroaster, who has been banished from the Bactrian empire, is seen dwelling on Mount Taurus where he has tought his doctrines to the savages, who have become deeply attached to him. To their deep chagrin, he leaves them to follow a voice that bids him deliver his country from Abramano's tyranny.

69

"In the third act Zoroaster appears at the walls of Bactria, while the people come out to meet him. Erinice seeks to kill Amelita, but Zoroaster protects her, and despite all Abramano's efforts she remains free. Before his departure Zoroaster entrusts her to the care of the elemental spirits.

"In the fourth act Abramano and Erinice with their followers are seen in an underground temple, where they offer sacrifices to Arimanius, the spirit of evil. Vengeance, Hatred, and the Furies appear to pledge their support to Abramano in the destruction of Zoroaster.

"In the fifth act Zoroaster and Amelita are seen on one side, Abramano and Erinice on the other, each party attended by its followers. The former invoke Oromazes, the spirit of goodness, the latter Arimanius, the spirit of evil. But signs appear in the heavens and in the end Abramano and Erinice with their followers succumb. Zoroaster and Amelita marry to public acclamation, whereupon peace and quiet once more descend on the empire.

"*Protestation*:

"All in this tragedy that runs counter to the teachings of Christianity must be seen in the light of words and deeds of people still engulfed in the errors of idolatry. Let the public rest assured that the author has selected his theme solely for the purpose of presenting a great display of scenery, dances, and stage spectacles."

The "protestation" reminds of a passage in Keyssler's travel record, in which he reports to his master: "It should be noted that in the Italian operas the authors preface the printed text with an explicit protestation of their pure Catholic faith, insisting that terms appearing in the text, such as *idolo, numi, deita, fato, fortuna, adorare,* etc., are to be regarded as no more than pious jests."

The review in the *Dresdener gelehrte und politische Anzeiger* of February 15, 1752, read: "The tragedy *Zoroaster,* performed during the carnival season at the Royal Theater in Dresden, deserves special attention on account of the excellent production, the fine decorations, the music, and the dancing."

Casanova himself reports: "Soon afterward I left Dresden. I left behind my dear mother and my sister, who had married the Court Piano Tutor Peter August. He had died two years before, leaving his widow and family in comfortable circumstances." This brother-in-law of Casanova's had been organist at the catholic church in Dresden, and he left a number of piano compositions in manuscripts now preserved at the State Library at Dresden.

CHAPTER NINE

PRAGUE AND THE IMPRESARIO
LOCATELLI

CASANOVA'S memoirs tell us that he went from Dresden to Prague, which was but a few hours journey from the capital of Saxony. He did not intend to tarry at the Bohemian capital. He paid a visit to the impresario Locatelli, for whom he had a letter, and for the rest lived with a Mrs. Morelli whom he loved and where for two or three days he found everything his heart desired. I do not know who this Morelli woman really was, but I suspect that she was the actress Teresa Morelli who later married the famous comedian and impresario Felix von Kurtz-Bernardon.

Casanova tells us about Locatelli, a very resourceful man whose acquaintance it was well worth while to make. "Every day," the adventurer reports, "his table was laid for thirty persons, and his guests were for the most part his professional associates—actors and actresses, dancers and friends. He presided at these delicious meals with great dignity, for good food was a passion with him."

Giovanni Battista Locatelli was an Italian of Casanova's own stripe, a man in whom musical talent was coupled with the urge for self-assertion and adventure. Born somewhere in Italy in 1715, he became the first private opera and ballet entrepreneur in Russia He played a most significant part in the history of the opera in Russia. Locatelli had been cast up in Russia at an early age, in 1733. He founded a theatrical enterprise but found that there was little patronage for the drama. Hence he joined a scholarly expedition titled *La Croyère* which penetrated as far as Kazan. There he was arrested as a suspicious character by the governor, "suffering much hardship and ill-treatment, being sent back and robbed by soldiers and subalterns in good Muscovite fashion," as Barthold tells us in his book on the historic personages in Casanova's life. "The Italian," Barthold continues, "vented his rancor at inhospitable Scythia in the so-called *Lettres Muscovites* which appeared in Paris in 1736."

Having left inhospitable Russia, Locatelli, adventurer of the stage, went to the Elector's court at Cologne in the capacity of opera director. For many years the two primadonnas Giovanna della Stella and Rosa Costa had graced the Cologne stage. The later ultimately married Torelli, a Neapolitan. But as for Giovanna, she became Locatelli's wife. She was reputed to have had a liaison with the Elector of Cologne, causing the prince to repair to Rome to purge himself of evil suspicion. In Brühl Palace near Cologne there still hangs a portrait of the handsome Giovanna Locatella, as she was called after her marriage.

The couple went to Prague, where Locatelli directed Italian opera in the Kotzen Theatre for almost a decade. He was enormously active and successful, and under his aegis Italian opera flourished in Prague as never before. He left Prague with the reputation of being one of the most progressive cities in the world, so far as the theater is concerned —a reputation that endured down to the days of Angelo Neumann, the Wagner enthusiast.

Locatelli invited Gluck and performed Gluck's opera *Ezio* in 1750. That same year the Empress Maria Theresa and her consort Francis I were encamped at Kolin. Locatelli staged the opera *Zenobia* in the camp, and the performance became a musical event of the first rank. He wrote librettos himself and there is some evidence that he was also a composer. I managed to unearth a libretto by Locatelli in the Castle Library at Raudnitz in Bohemia. The title page reads as follows::

"Diana nelle Selve. Componimento Drammatico da reppresentarsi in Musica nelle Elettorale Corte il 23 Novembre 1745 per Festiggiare il Glorioso Nome

di Sua Altezza Serenissima Elettorale Clemente Augusto Arcievesco di Colonia, Prencipe ed Elettore di Sacro Romano Imperio. La Poesia del Sig. Gio Battista Locatelli."

At the time Casanova was visiting Prague, Locatelli's contract with the Prag *Gubenium* was about to expire. He applied for an extension, which was granted in April 1753. But his career had passed its prime. A keen rival had arisen in the person of Joseph Kurtz-Bernardon, who soon enlisted Prague audiences on the side of "German comedy." Locatelli went into debt and was unable to meet his obligations even after a brief guest engagement at Dresden in 1755. In vain he sought permission to stage masquerade festivals. Then, suddenly, in 1757, Prague was besieged. The Kotzen Theatre sustained serious damage and the building was pillaged. Locatelli took advantage of the occasion to turn his back on Prague, escaping to St. Petersburg. As late as 1767 a document at Prague referred to him as "having fled to Russia."

When Casanova visited St. Petersburg later on, he found the onetime theater expert running a restaurant. "Minister Alsuvieff invited me to dine at Locatelli's at the *Katherinenhof.* This was an imperial countryseat which the Czarina had granted the aged stage director for life. He was surprised to see me, and I was even more surprised to see that he was running a restaurant. He served an excellent

75

meal to all comers, at a cost of one ruble, not including wine. . . ."

The old showman had met with little luck in Russia on this occasion as well. Despite the recommendations of Count Keyserling (to whom Johann Sebastian Bach dedicated his "Goldberg Variations"), he had gone into bankruptcy at Moscow in 1767. It was then that imperial favor granted him the historic *Krasny Kabak* or "red tavern" at the *Katherinenhof,* where he staged exquisite banquets for the aristocratic world.

CHAPTER TEN

VIENNA AND METASTASIO

FROM Prague Casanova went on to Vienna. He anticipated many advantages for himself there. He was eager to exploit his personality, his brilliance, his luck with women and at the gaming table. Vienna was a focus of political, social, and cultural life. Where else could an adventurer like Casanova make his fortune, if not in Vienna? The wealth of the world was amassed there, at the meeting place of the elect. Casanova was twenty-eight years old at the time, well equipped—as he himself puts it—but a little short of cash!

He carried a letter of recommendation. True, it was not in the line of his amorous adventures, yet it did bid fair to open the doors of Vienna's aristocracy to him. The letter in his pocket was from the pen of the Dresden librettist Giovanni Ambrosio Migliavacca, and it was adressed to the librettist

Pietro Metastasio, the imperial Austrian poet laureate. Migliavacca himself was but an imitator of the great Metastasio. He had held his post at Dresden since 1752, producing the opera *Soliman* by Hasse and also writing the libretto for Gluck's opera *Thetis*. As for Metastasio, he had been in Vienna since 1730, called there by the Countess Althann, the mistress of Emperor Charles VI and a patroness of the arts. The story went that Metastasio was secretly married to the Countess.

It is difficult today to fathom the full significance Metastasio held for the history of the opera, indeed, for the cultural history of Italy in general. In the words of his contemporary and critic, Eximeno, the *dolcezza*, the grace and sensitivity of his poetry, became the source that fed the entire operatic music of the late baroque age, a music instinct with beauty. It was but natural that Casanova, who had tried his own hand at writing librettos, was eager to make the acquaintance of this strange man. He tells us that he presented Migliavacca's letter to Metastasio immediately upon his arrival, and that he spent hours in conversation with the poet.

"Metastasio," Casanova relates, "was so modest that in the beginning I looked on his modesty as unnatural. But I was soon convinced that it was wholly genuine, for when he recited his verses, he was the first to draw attention to good passages and fine points. He did so with the same simplicity with which he pointed out his weaknesses."

The talk veered to Metastatio's teacher J. V. Gravina, outstanding Italian jurist and man of letters, and Metastasio recited some verses he had composed on the occasion of Gravina's death—Gravina had been his adopted father. "Touched by the memory of the loss of his friend and by the sweetness of his own verses, his eyes filled with tears as he spoke. When he had done, he asked me in a tone of touching simplicity: *'Ditemi il vero, si può dir' meglio?'* ["Tell me in truth whether it could have been said better."] I replied that he alone could think that possible. I then asked him whether his fine poetry cost him much effort. He showed me four or five pages with writing. Many lines were crossed out. The whole poem was only fourteen lines long, and he assured me that he had never been able to do more in one day. Thus he confirmed something I already knew, namely that it is precisely those verses which the average reader thinks of as having been written without effort that take the greatest amount of work.

" 'Which of your operas do you like best?' I asked him.

" *'Attilio Regolo, ma questo non vuol già dire, che sia il migliore.'*

" 'All of your works have been translated into

French prose in Paris, but the publisher [Richelet] has ruined himself in the process, for it is impossible to read them. This proves the loftiness and power of your poetry. . . .'

"He thereupon told me that he had never written an arietta without setting it to music himself, though ordinarily he showed his music to no one. 'It is a strange thing,' he continued, 'that the French should believe that verses can be adapted to music already written.' "

It may be in order to mention a few of Burney's remarks. Burney visited Metastasio in Vienna in 1772.

"The whole tenor of his life," Burney writes, "is equally innoxious with his writings. He lives with the most mechanical regularity, which he suffers none to disturb; he has not dined from home these thirty years; he is very difficult of access, and equally averse to new persons, and new things; he sees, in a familiar way, but three or four people, and them, constantly every night, from eight o'clock till ten; he abhors writing, and never sets pen to paper but by compulsion: as it was necessary to bind Silenus, before he would sing; and Proteus, to oblige him to give oracles.

"He has long been invested with the title and appointments of imperial laureate; and when the Emperor, Empress, or any one of the imperial family orders it, he sits down and writes, two hours at

a time only, just as he would transcribe a poem
written by any one else; never waiting for a call,
invoking the Muse, or even receiving her favours
at any other than his own stated periods."

The Englishman's remarks show a certain dis-
crepancy when compared to the picture sketched
by Casanova, yet in one respect at least Burney
lends support to Casanova:

"He was applied to by the editors of the *Ency-
clopédie,* to write the article *Opera* for that work;
but he politely declined the task, supposing it impossible that his sentiments on the subject should
be pleasing to the French nation."

As was but natural, Casanova at once established
connections in the Viennese theater. He attended
an opera rehearsal, there to meet the dancer Bodin
whom he knew from Turin. He also met Bodin's
beautiful wife, Mme. Geoffroi-Bodin. In 1752 she
had been engaged for the Vienna stage at the sizable
salary of 5,775 gulden. Both were famous solo dancers, and their names appear frequently in Viennese
memoirs. Khevenhüller's diary, for example, reports
that in 1766 Mme. Geoffroi "had herself left the
theater in disgust shortly before the departure of
Conte Durazzo." Many years later Casanova was to
meet the fair Mme. Geoffroi-Bodin at Orleans.

In Vienna Casanova also met the dancer Campi-
oni, husband of another dancer and notorious courtesan, Ancilla Cardini, from whom he was in the

process of obtaining a divorce. In his memoirs Casanova had presented her to his readers as the most famous courtesan in Venice, four years before the events just described. Among other noteworthy theatrical acquaintances Casanova made at the time, was the famous Victoria Tesi (1700-1775), possessor of one of the most renowned alto voices of all time. She was then already past her prime, but was still accounted a world prodigy because of the beauty and volume of her voice. As late as November 4, 1749, she sang the lead in Jomelli's *Dido*. Metastasio heard and admired her at the time, writing that she had made him feel twenty years younger. Dittersdorf gives much space to her in his autobiography. He tells us that the great librettist, "carried away by the extraordinary power of her acting," had expressly written his *Zenobia, Didone* and *Semiramide* for her. She celebrated her greatest triumphs at the Court of Spain, together with Farinelli. La Tesi died in Vienna, leaving a great fortune to her husband Tramontini, her former hairdresser and one of the many Italian adventurers in Vienna. The story went that she had unselfishly married him to avoid marriage to an aristocrat who was in love with her. Her declining years were spent in the home of the Prince of Saxe-Hildburghausen, an Austrian general and a great friend of music. Gluck and Dittersdorf lived in his palace as well.

La Tesi frequently sang at the house concerts staged by the Prince.

His acquaintance with Tesi enabled Casanova to introduce several of his friends to the Prince. Among these was an adventurer, Afflisio, who had once been nicknamed *Beppo il Cadetto*. He was a Neapolitan, and Casanova had encountered him the year before as a cardsharp. The Prince gave Afflisio captain's rank and he later became head of the *Burgtheater*, succeeding Count Durazzo. On another occasion Casanova again met Afflisio at Bologna, where he was a stage director. Later he sank step by step, dying a wretched death as a galley slave.

Another acquaintance of Casanova's was the famous Milan dancer Fogliazzi who later married the choreographer and dancer Gaspare Angiolini. He was a native Milanese, born in 1723, had performed in Florence and from 1748 to 1750, under the name of *C. Angiolini di Firenze,* at Venice. Later he appeared at Turin, and after many tours he was engaged in 1757 as successor to the famous Hilverding at Vienna. He was a brilliant choreographer, a proponent of the dramatic and expressive style of dancing brought to the stage by Noverre. The magnificent ballets in Gluck's *Don Juan*—which had such an important influence on Mozart's *Don Giovanni*—were created by Angiolini. He himself danced the part of Don Juan in this ballet in 1761,

Mme. Geoffroi-Bodin taking the part of Donna Elvira. He also created the ballets for Gluck's *Orfeo*.

Casanova fell desperately in love with Mme. Angiolini-Fogliazzi, but on this occasion he was truthful enough to admit that his love remained unrequited. The dancer was already in love with her paramour and later husband Angiolini, which aroused Casanova to these contemplations:

"A lady of the theater already in love with someone represents an impregnable fortress, unless one is able to build a bridge of gold. But I was not rich. Nevertheless I did not give up hope but continued to burn incense at her altar. She liked my company, for she used to show me the letters she wrote and I praised them for their beauty. She had a miniature likeness of herself—a likeness that was really striking. Irked over my wasted time and my lovesick follies, I decided, on the eve of my departure, to steal the portrait. Poor solace for a lover! Paying my final call, I saw the treasure lying about. I pocketed it and went on to Bratislava. . . ."

Later on, in Venice, our hero returned the picture to Fogliazzi, through the mediation of Giovanni Grimani, presumably the owner of San Giovanni Chrysostomo, where Angiolini had once appeared as a dancer. The ballerina had written Grimani in guarded terms that she suspected Casanova of the theft. Casanova's passion had evaporated. He surrendered the portrait with nonchalance. . . .

CHAPTER ELEVEN

PARIS AND THE NETHERLANDS

WE find little material bearing on literature and music in the two chapters of Casanova's life story that are least supported by historical evidence—his love affair with the nun M. M. at Venice; and the famous escape from the Leads of Venice—the notorious lead-roofed prison of the Doges.

He relates that he attended the opera in the *Teatro San Samuele* on one occasion in company of the fair nun. But after the second ballet they repaired to the *Ridotto* for the gaming. Nor do the literary discourses in which Casanova engaged with his nun in any sense have reference to medieval scholasticism or the church fathers, far less to theology. They deal with the sonnets of Pietro Aretino on Raimondi's engravings after Giulio Romano, describing the various "positions" in the art of love. They also deal with the *Conversation Between Maddalena and Giulio,* commonly attributed to Aretino under the title of *La Putana errante* and one of the reasons for his bad reputation. The dialogue is highly frivolous and like the sonnets it describes the "thirty-five positions," some of them utterly foolish. It was scarcely suitable literature for a nun! Casanova never forgot this love affair, in which the later Cardinal and French diplomat Pierre de Bernis played a very dubious role. It pervaded his whole life at the time.

Nevertheless, he manages to tell us that he made the acquaintance of Marcantonio Zorzi, a patrician who was a passionate friend of the theater and himself wrote a comedy that was a failure on the stage. Zorzi stubbornly insisted that Pietro Chiari, another writer of comedies, was at the bottom of his literary misfortune. Casanova, high in the favor of Zorzi and especially of Zorzi's beautiful wife, wrote epigrams that derided Chiari's comedies. This, in turn, earned him the hatred of another patrician, Condulmer, who was part owner of the *Teatro San Angelo* for which Chiari wrote, and who fancied that this unwelcome criticism of the plays performed at his theater did him injury. To Casanova's misfortune this Condulmer became a member of the "Council of Ten" and Inquisitor of State, and it was to him that Casanova attributed his later arrest and incarceration in the Leads. If this be true, Casanova was on this occasion, as on many others, a victim of his predilection for literay mockery.

Casanova paid dearly for his escapades in Venice.

86

PLATE 7.   La Camargo, Famous French Dancer (After a Painting by Lancret)

PLATE 8.

La Visita al Convento by Francesco Guardi (1712-1793)

Cast into prison, he succeeded in making good his escape only by the most adventurous means. His escape from the Leads of Venice became famous, and his account of it was reprinted innumerable times. The time he spent behind bars was scarcely very productive for our purposes. Poor Casanova, put on rations of bread and water, had little time to give to music and the theater. His one thought was how he might escape from the hell of the Leads.

When he had accomplished his escape, he turned toward Paris. The first visit he paid there was to the home of his friend Sylvia Balletti, whose real name was Benozzi. She had four children, of whom the charming Manon Balletti had quite captured Casanova's heart. As has already been mentioned, he was officially betrothed to her, and a series of exquisite letters from her to the Don Juan of Venice has been preserved.

There was much music at the Balletti house. "Manon owned a clavicembalo, three guitars, a violin and a mandolin. When she later married the architect Blondel, her marriage contract mentioned a clavicembalo, painted in green and gilt, a harp with case, two guitars, and a violin."

When Casanova first met Manon she was engaged to the musician Clement, who had been giving her piano lessons for three years. This was probably Charles François Clement who, according to Eitner's source-book, was born in 1720 in the Provence and who practiced the profession of music teacher in Paris. An opera, *La Bohémienne,* some piano pieces, and a treatise on the art of accompaniment from the pen of this unsuccessful rival of Casanova's have been preserved.

Naturally there were other actresses and singers who aroused Casanova's interest. He made the acquaintance of Jeanette Françoise Quinault, famous for her performance of *Phaedra.* Camilla, an actress at the *Comédie,* who offered him her house on the *Barrière Blanche,* became another of the adventurer's favorites. There he came to know the Count Tour d'Auvergne, who in turn introduced him to Mme. d'Urfé, his aunt, insanely addicted to alchemy and clairvoyance. Casanova later exploited this addiction in the most brazen manner, living on this woman's lunacy for years.

This section of his memoirs shows with special clarity how depraved theatrical life was in Paris at the time. "I was chiefly preoccupied," he writes, "with those women who belonged to the public by virtue of the fact that they were singers or dancers or played queens and chambermaids on the stage night after night. They laid claim to good manners, but they also demanded great liberties and enjoyed their so-called independence by yielding to *Amor* and *Pluto* in turn, and often to both at once. It is not very difficult to strike up an acquaintance with these priestesses of joy and profligacy, and so I entrenched myself with several of them. The foyers of the theaters are bazaars where lovers practice their talents in spinning out amorous intrigues, and I made tolerable progress in this noble school."

In the time from October 1758 to January 1759 Casanova visited the Netherlands, allegedly on a diplomatic mission. He claims to have met with the most diverse adventures in the field of finance, love, and mystery. Gugitz (in his book, *Giacomo Casanovas Lebensroman*) examined them carefully and relegated most of them to the realm of Casanova's imagination.

In company with his young Dutch friend Esther, Casanova attended a concert at Amsterdam: "Following a fine symphony, a violin concerto, and an oboe concerto, there appeared the famous Italian singer they called Mme. Trenti." In her Casanova recognized one of his youthful loves, Teresa Imer, wife of the dancer Pompeati. He rightly insisted that this woman, who had played such an important part in his life, could have well written memoirs worthy to be compared with his own. Gugitz discusses at length the life of this once famous singer, who later became a theatrical entrepreneuse. In Amsterdam Casanova heard her sing an aria beginning with these words: *"Eccoti giunta alfin, donna infelice!"* They were words that seemed to have been written expressly for the occasion.

A curious sidelight is thrown on the treatment

then still accorded artists by Casanova's report that the singer "received no remuneration except what the listeners placed on the plate" with which she passed through their rows. " 'Are her earnings substantial?' " Casanova asked the fair Esther. " 'I doubt it, for the audience has already paid admission. If she gets thirty or forty gulden it will be much. The day after tomorrow she will be at The Hague, a day later at Rotterdam, and then she will return here. She has been leading this life for more than six months and one always listens to her with pleasure.' " Such was the reply by the spoiled Esther who seems to have known something about music.

Dittersdorf makes mention of Pompeati himself in his autobiography. He was "in his younger years one of the leading solo dancers, but as he grew older he left the theater and gave lessons in dancing and also in the Italian language." In both subjects Dittersdorf was his eager pupil. From Dresden the young couple had come to London, where, on January 7, 1746, Teresa had appeared as *seconda donna* in Gluck's opera, *La Caduta de giganti*. In the fall of 1746 La Pompeati was again engaged at Vienna, Khevenhüller noting in his diary for December 8: "The show [Hasse's *Alessandro nelle Indie*] was so poor and so confused on account of the absence of one of the characters (the singer Pompeati having been overtaken with labor pains as she entered the theater) that I was ashamed." At the time the singer was delivered of her son Joseph, later to be claimed by Casanova as his own son, the little Count Aranda, and still later to play a part in the notorious affair of Mme. d'Urfé.

CHAPTER TWELVE

TERESA POMPEATI

IT is in order for us to trace the story of this once famous singer. We already know who she was. She was the young girl whom Casanova had met as a young man in the Venice home of Senator Malipiero—he had just returned to his native city from Padua. The young libertine had forfeited the favor of the influential Senator, when Malipiero had caught him in a compromising situation with little Teresa, daughter of the theatrical manager Imer and then sixteen years old. As a matter of fact, Casanova had been soundly caned.

Teresa too followed the theater. She had appeared in London, as a member of the famed Mingotti opera troupe in 1748, and later with the same company in Copenhagen. Here she had been in good company. A newspaper clippping tells us "that such an excellent cast has never before been seen in one place, the four finest voices in all Italy here

being met together. In addition to the famous Mme.
Turcotti and M. Casati, Mesdames Birckerin and
Pompeati . . . have been engaged from London. M.
Gluck, renowned for his musical skill, is now conductor in place of M. Scalambrini. . . ."
Information about the Mingotti company
emerges from the correspondence that passed between an artist couple named Pircker, preserved in
the state archives at Stuttgart and excerpted by
Erich H. Müller in a study of the subject. What
chiefly interests us are certain passages that show
La Pompeati as being on friendly terms with none
less than Gluck, whom she knew from London.
Mme. Pircker was bitterly jealous of Teresa's successes.

"Rehearsal today," she writes to her husband,
"rehearsal tomorrow, and the day after tomorrow
the first performance, *Bajazet*. You can get an idea
of how poisonous the fat one is. She hasn't even
showed up yet." "The fat one" refers to Teresa
Pompeati. Soon afterward we read: "We're fast
friends again, I and the fat one. At least she pretends to be." Another letter contains mysterious
hints about the singer Beccheroni: "Serves her
right, for inflicting such harm on poor Gluch
[Gluck]." La Pircker adds that she would be only
too willing to avenge "Klug" (Gluck). Evidently
the matter had to to do with a troublesome ailment
that afflicted Gluck, for we read: "I've regretted a

thousand times that I ever told you about Klug's sickness. For God's sake, don't tell anyone."

The husband reassured his indiscreet wife and fed her vanity by passing adverse judgment on La Pompeati and her art: "Don't worry about Gluck's trouble. No one has learned what you wrote me about it. As far as Pompeati is concerned, his partiality won't do much good, for according to what you write and what Abacco and Giacomozzi have told me, her singing holds no danger. It's too capricious, they all agree." Later on Mme. Pircker wrote: "Thank God Pompeati has departed. I never in my life saw a woman so bent on intrigue."

Teresa had returned to Hamburg. In Holberg's letters, which are classical Danish source material on music, her name is found beside those of Giovanna della Stella and Rosa Costa, singers we know from Prague. Somewhat later we find La Pompeati in Bayreuth, where she became the chosen favorite of Margrave Frederic. Gugitz demonstrates that Casanova's data on his old friend are not in full agreement with the historical facts. Casanova writes: "In 1753 I had seen her [Teresa] in Venice, and at the time we had taken each other a little more seriously. She then departed for Bayreuth, where she became the mistress of the Margrave. I had promised to visit her, but C. C. and my fair nun M. M. left me with neither the time nor the desire. Soon afterward the

Leads engulfed me, and I had other things to think of besides redeeming a promise."

From Bayreuth Teresa had gone to Paris, where she led the life of a great lady, but later on Paris grew too hot for her because of the debts she had incurred, and she went to Belgium. Casanova tells us that there Prince Charles Alexander of Lorraine granted her a monopoly on running theaters in the Austrian Netherlands. "It was a huge enterprise, causing her enormous expense. By and by she was compelled to sell her diamonds and laces, and in the end she had to flee to the Netherlands to avoid being thrown into prison."

Thus Casanova met her at Amsterdam in rather desperate circumstances. He at once took her little son, the so-called Count of Aranda, with him to Paris, later exploiting the lad for his own selfish purposes with the mystery-mongering madwoman d'Urfé. Teresa, on her part, met a certain Cornelys in the Netherlands and went with him to London, where she initially gave concerts under the name of Mme. Cornelys and later staged magnificent festivities. She was a worthy companion to Casanova! We shall revert to her in a later chapter.

It is not known how long the Pompeati couple remained together. He became assistant director of the German Ballet at Vienna, where he created a series of ballets, as he did at Venice. He died a violent death. The Vienna *Diarium* reports on March 23, 1768: "Angelus Pompeati, dancer at the German Theater, wounded himself mortally in a fit of madness. An inquest was held by the court at the old *Haarmarkt*. The deceased was fifty-five years old." At any rate, the dancer seems to have died a divorced man.

CHAPTER THIRTEEN

RETURN TO PARIS

IN February 1759 Casanova returned to Paris. In the Netherlands he had conducted financial transactions profitable to the French Government. This had both earned him a great deal of money and given him a certain reputation in Paris society. He continued to lead his wonted profligate life.

Music was by no means slighted. In the company of his fiancée, Manon Balletti, he attended the concerts staged by the wealthy tax farmer, Alexander Jean-Joseph le Riche de la Poplinière, at Passy. Poplinière was an amateur musician, a student of Rameau, and maintained a private theater. Of significance to the history of music is the fact that in 1751 he engaged Gossec as director of his concerts. It was he, too, who presented to the Paris public Johann Stamitz, the great reformer in orchestral music. On Stamitz's advice, Poplinière added to his orchestra horns, clarinets and later a harp, an instrument that had not heretofore been employed in the orchestra. He himself wrote a number of arias, a few of which Rameau included with his own works.

When Casanova made his acquaintance, the tax farmer was unsuccessfully wooing Mlle. X. C. V., a lady with whom Casanova was engaged in rather scandalous intrigues and who has been identified by Casanova scholars as Giustina Wynne. She was a well-known author at the time and even Goethe knew her novel, *Les Morlaques.* It was during this period that Casanova also visited Jean Jacques Rousseau. He met the philosopher in the company of that same wealthy Mme. d'Urfé, whose preoccupation with mysticism and alchemy he exploited so shamelessly, as has been already mentioned.

"We rode to Montmorency to pay him a visit on the pretext of giving him some music to copy. He did this work exquisitely. His fees were twice those of other copyists, but in return his execution was beyond reproach. At the time the famous writer was earning his living in this fashion." As is known, the French philosopher was eager to make himself independent of his friends by earning his own living as a music copyist. The German music historian Johann Nikolaus Forkel (*Musikalisch-kritische Bibliothek,* III, 336) reports that another of Rousseau's visitors, Count Falkersheim, was likewise amazed to see Rousseau, the author of so many eminent works, "presently preoccupied with writing and copying music." Well, Rousseau was not merely a philosopher. He is of considerable importance in the history of French music, not merely as the author of the famous *Dictionnaire de Musique,* but also as the composer of several operas. His song play, *Le Devin du Village,* held its place in the repertory for sixty years and was a factor in Mozart's *Bastien and Bastienne.*

Another musical event related by Casanova is a visit to an oratorio performance given in the Tuileries. "A motet composed by Mondonville was being given. The text was by *Abbé* Voisenon, to whom I had supplied the theme." At another place the Venetian reports: "Under my influence the *Abbé* resolved to write oratorios in verse. They were sung for the first time at the Tuileries, on days when the theaters were closed for religious reasons." It appears that these statements by Casanova are correct. For Fétis, in his *Biographie universelle des musiciens,* likewise mentions Mondonville's oratorio, placing the time of its conception between 1758 and 1759. Rousseau himself was delighted with Mondonville's motets. He writes: *Les Français réussissent bien dans ce genre de musique. Leurs motets sont beaux et bien travaillés. Ceux du célèbre Lalande sont des chefs d'oeuvres en ce genres et les motets de M. Mondonville tout pétillants de génie et de feu, charment aujourd'hui les amateurs de la nouvelle musique."* It is quite possible that Casanova had his share in the history of the French oratorio. He was a Jack-of-all trades, who knew everything, tried everything, had his finger in everything. Why should he not have tried to shine in this field as well?

CHAPTER FOURTEEN

STUTTGART

FROM March 15 to April 2, 1760, we find Casanova in Stuttgart, where Duke Charles Eugene maintained a brilliant court. This Prince sought to emulate Louis XV. His thoughts were centered wholly on show and dissipation, and his household devoured vast sums of money which he raised by placing intolerable financial burdens on his subjects. Yet his bent for luxury did make significant contributions to the development of music in the eighteenth century.

The pride of cultural life at Stuttgart was Noverre's ballet. It was in the very year in which Casanova visited Stuttgart that the Duke of Württemberg had attracted Jean Georges Noverre, great reformer of the ballet, to his court. Here Noverre created his world-famous ballets, for which the composers Deller and Rudolph wrote the music. But even the spendthrift Duke Charles Eugene was unable to defray the expenses of the enterprise and Noverre thus had to turn his back on the Württemberg capital. Stuttgart also boasted the Italian composer Nicola Jomelli, who was called the "Italian Gluck" and was one of the greatest opera composers of the eighteenth century.

Let us listen to Casanova's own words on his theatrical impressions: "The Duke maintained French comedy, serious and comic Italian opera, and twenty Italian dancers, each of whom had been in his time leading dancer at one of the great theaters of Italy. Noverre was his choreographer and ballet director. At times Noverre employed more than a hundred characters. A skilled master technician and the best scene painters rivaled each other, at great expense, in making the spectators believe in magic. The dancers were all pretty, and each one boasted of having made her lord and master happy on at least one occasion. The Prima Ballerina came from Venice—she was the daughter of a gondolier named Gardella."

It is a curious thing that time and again Casanova encountered childhood friends and playmates among the singers and dancers he saw on the stage. This time it was La Gardella, onetime protégée of the aged Senator Malipiero, who had so soundly caned the young Casanova when he had been caught in a compromising situation, making love to another protégée, little Teresa Imer, later the singer

Pompeati and still later the English impresaria Mme. Cornelys.

Gardella's husband was Michael del Agatha. Together with the famous choreographer Sauveterre, he had, in 1758, founded the Opera and Comedy Ballet at Stuttgart, thus becoming Noverre's predecessor. (Sittard, *Zur Geschichte der Musik & des Theaters am Württembergischen Hofe*, II, 59.)

Casanova reports that the Duke found Mme. d'Agatha to his taste and "requested her of her husband." The husband accounted himself fortunate to be able to cede his wife. But a year later the Duke had tired of her charms and pensioned her with the title of "Madame." The story the adventurer tells of this dancer is characteristic of the depraved atmosphere that prevailed at the theaters of the petty German courts of the time:

"The title 'Madame' which D'Agatha had been granted aroused the jealousy of all the other dancers. Each one thought she had the necessary qualities to become the acknowledged mistress, all the more so, since La Gardella merely had the title and the stipend. They all intrigued against her, but the Venetian woman possessed the power to fascinate to a high degree and was able to maintain her place despite all the cabals. Far from reproaching the Duke with his constant infidelities, she encouraged him, and since she did not love him, she was glad that he neglected her, leaving her to spend her time

103

in her own fashion. She derived the greatest satisfaction from the fact that all the dancers who aspired to become the Duke's mistress, came to her to recommend their charms. She received them in friendly fashion, counseled and encouraged them in making themselves agreeable to the Prince. He on his part found her tolerance admirable and convenient and regarded himself as obliged to show her his gratitude. In public he deferred to her as though to a Princess."

Naturally Casanova attended the opera soon after his arrival in Stuttgart. He reports that the Duke admitted the public to the fine theater without charge. "The Prince sat facing the orchestra," his memoirs tell us, "surrounded by his splendid court. I took my seat in a box in the lowest circle, alone and quite content to be able to give my undivided attention to a musical piece by the famous Jumella [sic!], who was in the service of the Duke. Unfamiliar with the customs at certain petty German courts, I applauded a solo, exquisitely sung by a certain *castrato* whose name I have forgotten." Casanova's remark refers to the rule that was enforced at many German courts, to the effect that no one could applaud until the Prince had shown his approval. Presumably Casanova desired to attract a little attention. In this he succeeded. Immediately after he had applauded "a man stepped into my box and said something to me in a rude tone. All I could reply was 'nicht verstanden.' The man left and soon afterward an officer appeared. He told me in excellent French that the sovereign was in the theater and hence it was not permitted to applaud. 'Very well, sir, I shall return when the sovereign is not present. For when I like an aria, I cannot refrain from expressing my approval.' "

Casanova had scarcely left the theater, when he was overtaken by another officer who told him that the Duke wished to see him. He had achieved what he wanted. The Duke was gracious and even permitted him to applaud as often as he wanted. But Casanova made no use of this license, for he now found the singing mediocre—presumably even the bravura arias of the castrato he had liked so much before.

We have not been able to determine with certainty the identity of the singer mentioned by Casanova. At the time these castrati were at the Württemberg court: Giuseppe Jozzi, Francesco Guerrieri, Giuseppe Aprile, and Pasquale Potenza. Burney, the renowned English music historian, reported in 1772 that there were fifteen eunuchs among the singers in the Military Academy at Ludwigsburg in Württemberg, "there being in the service of the Court two Bolognese surgeons highly skilled in performing this operation." It will be seen to what extremes the Duke's subjects had to submit!

The opera Casanova heard was Nicolo Jomelli's *Alessandro nelle Indie,* based on the libretto of the same title by Metastasio. This opera had been first performed on February 11, 1760 in celebration of the Duke's birthday. Readers desiring full information about the music and the text should consult the comprehensive book by Hermann Abert, *Jomelli as an Opera Composer,* which also mentions the ballets Casanova must have witnessed. Of these ballets the textbook says: "After the first act there was presented the ballet entitled *The Indians of the Empire of the Great Mogul;* and after the second, *Orpheus Descending into Hell to Seek His Beloved Eurydice and Finding Her at Last in the Elysian Fields Among the Happy Spirits.* After the third act there appeared nymphs, satyrs, and other deities, 'solemnly celebrating the marriage feast of Porus with Cleofide.' "

After the ballet the Duke retired to the box of his current favorite and an officer asked the Italian to go and pay his respects to "Madame" as well. Casanova was incautious enough to say that the dancer was his cousin, addressing her as such in the box. The next day, visiting her at her fine residence, he presumably continued to treat her in "cousinly" fashion. The dancer's mother found little pleasure in this "relationship" with Casanova. She came from the lowest class of Venice, and for many years her sister, a fat, blind beggarwoman, had her post on the Rialto bridge, but she now regarded herself as a cut above Casanova, because of her daughter's position at court. She forbade him to come to the house and caused him nothing but trouble at Stuttgart.

But Casanova found other dancers at Stuttgart, all of them very pretty and complaisant, and all of them old acquaintances. There was the Venetian dancer Binetti (on whose account he later had his famous duel with the Polish aristocrat Branicky in Warsaw). Anna Binetti was a pupil of Noverre's, had been a solo dancer in Venice, and was herself a fine choreographer. But at Stuttgart, at any rate, she did not show outstanding friendliness toward Casanova. Burney saw her at Padua, when she appeared there in the opera *Scipione in Carthago* by Locchini, together with the dancer Bic and the singers Potenza and Ettori. Casanova also met the dancer Guillaume Baletti, son of his old friend Sylvia. He was at the time married to the actress Vulcano, daughter of a comedian. Another old acquaintance was the violinist Andreas Kurz, who had been Casanova's colleague in Venice when the two had played at the *Teatro San Samuele*. Kurz introduced Casanova to his charming daughter, who was also a dancer, telling him with paternal pride: "She's not made for the Duke's beautiful eyes. He'll never get her." "Alas," Casanova continues, "the man was no prophet, for the Duke did get her soon afterward, indeed, she loved him. She bore him two little darlings, but even these tokens of love proved incapable of tying down the inconstant Prince."

Stuttgart was one of the cities the adventurer had to leave head over heels on account of his gambling and love affairs. His most loyal accomplices in his dire straits were his Italian women friends of the opera and the ballet.

CHAPTER FIFTEEN

REUNION WITH ITALY

BY way of Switzerland Casanova turned his steps toward Italy, the land for which he always yearned. Yet his fervent desire to visit the land of his birth did not prevent him from making an extensive stop-over in Switzerland. Despite its Puritan outlook, this country afforded the Italian the opportunity for engaging in scandalous affairs with seemingly respectable women.

The Calvinist austerity of the Swiss was conspicuous on every hand, even making itself felt in matters of music. The only musical intelligence Casanova provides is dated from Zurich, where he reports having attended a municipal concert: "I found the concert poor and was bored. The gentlemen all sat together on the right side, the ladies on the left." This, to be sure, was scarcely to Casanova's taste. There was no professional theater whatever in Switzerland at the time.

In Italy he was able to enjoy all the pleasures of

music and the theater without restraint, together
with the indulgences connected with them. But before he reached Italy, he made another stop-over
in southern France, visiting the opera in Avignon.
The Paris Opera had sent part of its personnel in
tour to southern France. On the playbill he saw the
name Astrandy. This was the famous dancer of the
Paris Opera who was reputed to have killed a whole
series of her lovers, including Count Egmont. The
following verses dealt with her:

> Quel spectacle affreux se présente
> Et dans les coeurs porte l'effroi?
> J'apperçois une ombre sanglante
> Qui traîne une fille après soi.
> Des trois scènes la noire cohorte
> L'accompagne et donne main forte
> A son implacable ennemi;
> Sous leur pas la terre s'entr'ouvre.
> Quel est l'objet que je découvre?
> Vite approchons—c'est Astrandy.

As it turned out, it was not this fair and blood-
thirsty dancer whom Casanova found in the theater
but her homely sister. He engaged in such shameless orgies with her and the hunchbacked actress
Lepi, that the reader's hair almost stands on end.

Soon afterward we find the adventurer at Genoa.
He found an excellent company of actors there and
conceived the urge to become a dramatic translator
and stage director. Thus he resolved to translate

Voltaire's *Ecossaise* into the Italian. He presented his translation to the theater director Pietro Rossi, a luminary of the Italian stage at the time. The historian of the theater Bartoli (*Notizie storiche de'Comici italiani,* Padova, 1782) tells us that Rossi was born about 1720, and was for many years attached to the theater of the Marchese degli Obizzi in Padua, where he entertained the whole city each carnival as a comedian. Later, according to Bartoli, he formed his own company, touring all the big cities of Italy and earning much applause and a great deal of money, until, in 1778, he retired with his family to Cento, to conduct, of all things, a grocery!

Rossi offered no objection when Casanova invited the actors to his home to read them his piece. Casanova's insight into matters of the theater emerges from the following passage in his memoirs: "I knew that lazy and indolent actors usually are concerned only about their own parts, never seeking to enter into the spirit of the whole play. Hence it often happens that a piece is presented poorly over all, even though the details are well rehearsed." He revealed the same understanding when he insisted that the play should be given without a prompter. The performance was actually a great success, and had to be repeated five times to sold-out houses.

From Genoa Casanova went to Pisa. Here he made the acquaintance of the famous impromptu actress Corilla. "When she sang," he relates, "she but had to fasten her squinting eyes on some man in order to make a conquest." Burney, under date of September 11, 1770, wrote from Florence that he had been introduced to the famous impromptu actress Sgra. Maddalena Morelli that very evening, and that afterward he had visited her in her home on frequent occasions. She was generally called La Corilla, and was likewise a pupil of Sgr. Nardini. Almost every night, according to Burney, she held a *conversazione* or *assemblée*, at which strangers and Florentine scholars were often present. Quite apart from her admirable talent for instantly speaking in verses on any topic and for playing violin ripienos at a concert, she could sing with great expressiveness and had a rather skilled throat, Burney stated.

La Corilla was born in Pistoia and lived in many cities—Rome, Leghorn, Florence, and Venice. Her great talent as an improviser is mentioned by Count Lamberg, Alexei Orlov, and Winckelmann. She was a member of the Arcadian Academy in Rome, where she was crowned as a poetess in 1771 under humiliating circumstances described among others by Casanova:

"The shouts of the people did not swerve a certain Cardinal of whom it was insisted that he entertained something more than friendship for the poetess. The Pope had given his consent. Corilla was crowned and jeered. The mob reviled her, while the poets sang her praises and the Cardinal made the presentation. She immediately left Rome and thereafter lived in Florence." This report is by the historian Archenholtz in his book *England and Italy.*

Casanova himself later reverts to Corilla, and his subject is again the coronation of the poetess, which took place at night at the Capitol. "Corilla should have been crowned in the daytime or not at all. It was ill-advised to pick the night. This clandestine coronation did little honor to the lady and discredited her admirers.." *Abbé* Pizzi, president of the Arcadian Academy, who was the main force behind the event, was flooded with jeering jingles and satires to such an extent that for several months he did not dare show his face in public.

Goethe too must have known Corilla, judging by his poem entitled *Reply by a Jew of Cortona to Corilla Who in Her Improvisations had Admonished Him to Embrace the Christian Faith.*

From Pisa the way led to Florence. Naturally Casanova's first visit was to the theater where he saw Rossi, the famous *Arlecchino,* whose reputation he found greater than his achievement. He passed the same judgment on the Florentine declamatory style, which found little favor with him. About the singer Pertici he said: "Now that he was old and could no longer sing, he played comedy, and very well indeed. This is a rare occurrence, for singers of

113

both sexes always think that they will keep their voices and consequently neglect the art of acting. Hence a common cold reduces their performance to complete mediocrity."

The next day Casanova attended the opera which was playing in the theater in the *Via della Pergola*. Here he had a delightful surprise. He discovered a singer with whom he had fallen desperately in love in his earliest youth. It had been in the year 1744 that he had come to the family of a comedian in Ancona, consisting of mother, two daughters, and two sons, one of the latter being palmed off as the *castrato* Bellino, though "he" was later revealed to be a girl. This girl, now appearing as a singer under the name of Teresa Lanti, was then at the peak of her fame. Casanova tells us that she had played an important part in the theatrical life of Naples from 1741 to 1757, while from 1760 to 1762 she had been primadonna at Florence. Strangely enough, her name appears in not a single history of the theater, though her portrait is in the Museum of the Theatre at Milan.

Teresa, on her part, had loved Casanova passionately; but now that she was married to young Palesi (she also called herself Palesi-Lanti), she told Casanova that she must keep her marriage vows. It was the kind of pious resolution that Casanova always ignored. There was an idyllic breakfast at the singer's home. She did not shrink from exchanging the most compromising caresses with him in the presence of her own husband. And she presented Casanova with their son, Cesare Filippo Lanti, whom she introduced as her brother and who was a finished pianist. The handsome youth was the spit and image of Casanova.

Then she told Casanova her story. The great *castrato* Salimbeni had been her first protector, later her lover. In 1741 this famous singer had placed her, dressed as a boy, with a woman in Bologna, promising to send for her in four years from Dresden. Teresa had thus scored her first success as the youth Bellino, as a *castrato* rather than a primadonna. The episode might almost be titled "From the Boyhood Years of a Girl." It was Casanova who had liberated her and made her again a woman. She vowed everlasting gratitude to him. Nor did she fail to make good her pledge. She offered him her whole fortune. . . .

The story shows once again how fast and loose Casanova played with historical dates. According to Teresa's story Salimbeni died in 1743 in the Tyrol. Actually he did not die until 1751, in Laibach, on a journey from Germany to Italy.

Casanova must have known Salimbeni in the flesh. A handwritten note in the Casanova archives at Hirschberg reads: "*Je me souviens de Carestini et du très noble Salimbeni, célèbres castrati, qui riaient bien lorsqu'ils trouvaient des innocents qui les pleignaient."*

Teresa occupied a dominant position. Singers came to her for rehearsal, which started as early as ten o'clock in the morning. She received them with exquisite grace, accepting the handkisses of all her guests. Casanova noted with great satisfaction that she enjoyed the highest prestige everywhere. But the rehearsal, which took three hours, bored him. At Teresa's house he made the acquaintance of an excellent singer from Parma, Redegonda, and also of the dancer Corticelli. Both of these women later played special roles in the life of our hero.

Redegonda was his mistress for some time. But he surrendered her to the wealthy English libertine Percy. She seems to have stuck to Englishmen henceforth, for a few years later we find her on intimate terms with the British General Salenmon at Wesel, whence, by the way, Casanova took her with him to Brunswick in his carriage. At Brunswick she became *seconda donna*—second leading lady—at the local theater managed by the impresario Nicolini and also the mistress of the Duke of Brunswick, a fact that did not prevent her from carrying on her amour with Casanova.

Corticelli, the other theatrical personage Casanova met at the house of Teresa Lanti, was from Bologna and but thirteen years old at the time, but it would appear that she too could look back on a world of experience. She had trouble with the theater director, a Jew, who had promised in the contract to let her dance a *Pas de deux* at the opera. This obligation he had failed to fulfill. Casanova resolved to obtain satisfaction for the youthful dancer. He interceded with the ballet master and the theater manager in an effort to have the girl perform her favorite dance. Pledges were made, but there was one delay after another. Casanova grew impatient and promised his servant twenty-five sequins for wreaking "gentlemanly vengeance" on the tardy Jewish theater manager. The servant laid an ambush one night and administered a sound beating to the poor wretch. Casanova took great pride in the exploit!

Somewhat later Casanova abducted the merry girl—she laughed the whole day long—to Bologna. They were followed by her avaricious mother—the prototype of the stage mother of the eighteenth century. Corticelli was about to depart for Prague where, so she told Casanova, she had been engaged as second ballerina. It is noteworthy that among the ballet personnel of the Prague theater director Kurtz-Bernardon we find a dancer named Maria Corticelli, who in the fall of 1761 appeared in the ballet in the opera *La Clemenza di Tito*, presumably composed by Jomelli or Giuseppe Scarlatti.

Casanova had her come from Prague to Paris. On

New-Year's Day of 1762 he wrote her that he would meet her and her mother at Metz and the meeting actually took place. Here Casanova's dates are quite accurate. But what did the old reprobate want with the dancer? For years he had been swindling the enormously wealthy and foolish old Frenchwoman Mme. d'Urfé with occultistic and cabbalistic humbug. Apparently he wanted to have done with the madwoman, whom he had led to believe that he would transform her into a man with the help of the cabala. For this purpose he required a "virgin neophyte," and he summoned Corticelli to Paris on the pretense that she enjoyed this virtue. It would lead us too far afield to trace the various phases of this farce. He surprised his "virgin neophyte," whom he had introduced to the rich Frenchwoman as "Countess Lascaris," in bed with the Basle canon, Count B. That was too much even for Casanova. He inquired of his "oracle" whether the operation for which he needed the virginal Countess Lascaris should now be performed. The oracle replied that she could not be used since she had been defiled by a "black demon" dressed as a priest. Casanova therefore dismissed the dancer with her mother, unquestionably paying them a pretty penny in hush money. . . .

One asks oneself why Casanova picked Corticelli for this, the greatest imposture of his career. Well, the dancer was gifted with a sense of humor. She

PLATE 9.   Count Waldstein's Castle at Dux, Where Casanova Spent His Last Days

JCOSAMERON

OU

HISTOIRE

D'EDOUARD,

ET

D'ELISABETH

qui passèrent quâtre vingts un ans chez les
Mégamicres habitans aborigénes du Protocosme
dans l'intérieur de notre globe, traduite
de l'anglois par

JACQUES CASANOVA

DE SEINGALT VÉNITIEN

Docteur ès loix Bibliothécaire de Monsieur le comte
de Waldstein seigneur de Dux Chambellan
de S. M. J. R. A.

A Prague à l'imprimerie de l'école normale.

PLATE 10.
Titlepage for *Icosameron*, the Utopian Novel Which
Casanova Published in His Old Age

was ready for anything, always in good spirits and deeply devoted to Casanova. It is a curious thing, but even after her betrayal Casanova ran across her again and again. He met her in Turin, though she was there commited to another paramour, and he had Dupré, who was there, give her dancing lessons (This Dupré is not to be confounded with the famous Duprès of Paris). Indeed, he actually kept her, until her colleague, the beautiful dancer Agatha, whom Casanova loved and coveted, made it a price of her surrender, that the adventurer should publicly renounce Corticelli. He then prevailed upon Dupré to stage a ball at which only professional dancers were to dance. The other ladies of Turin were to be but spectators. He danced all the quadrilles and a minuet with Agatha, thus slighting Corticelli. But not until he again caught the girl redhanded with another man did he finally renounce her. He met her once again in Paris, whither she had doubtless gone to exploit her acquaintance with the mystical Marquise. Casanova met her there, living in utter destitution and afflicted with a loathsome disease, of which she ultimately died. The typical life of a little dancer in the eighteenth century!

But let us get back to the year 1760 and Casanova's sojourn at Florence. It so happened that he was expelled from the city on account of an obscure financial matter. He went to Rome, and here we shall insert into our musical merry-go-round an episode that belongs rather to the field of the fine arts. This was Casanova's encounter with the art connoisseur and antiquarian Johann Joachim Winckelmann, whom he met in the house of the painter Raphael Mengs. Casanova's own brother Francesco, painter of battle scenes, was Mengs' assistant.

Casanova praises the lovable temperament of Winckelmann, who turned somersaults with Mengs' children on the floor. In the spirit of Anacreon and Horace, this learned sage joined happily in the carefree games of children. Of Mengs Casanova says that he never rose from the table except in an advanced state of intoxication, an observation that reminds us of Winckelmann's own remark in one of his "Letters" that everyone ought to drink beyond his thirst at least once a month.

Casanova does not tell us whether he enjoyed any musical or theatrical treats at Rome. He visited only the *Teatro Aliberti,* where, to use his own term, he found the opera "abominable." He thought better of it at Naples. He was interested in the *Teatro San Carlo* there more as a social than a musical institution. It would be most interesting, had Casanova left us his impressions of the operas that then being performed at Naples—operas by Piccini, Traetta, Logroscino, and others. But he barely touches upon the subject. "The young King sat in his box, surrounded by a court that was dressed resplendently but in poor taste. The pit and the loges were full. The latter are decorated with mirrors. On this particular evening, the occasion being some memorial celebration, the theater was brillantly illuminated." It must have been a memorable spectacle, but Casanova merely mentions that the glare impaired the effectiveness of the stage settings.

From Naples Casanova returned to Rome, but not without engaging in an adventure en route, with the singer of the Prince of Cassara, Diana. It was an unexpected affair. The rogue had announced a nocturnal visit to her pretty chambermaid. In place of the maid he found the less attractive singer, all prepared for an hour of dalliance. Casanova fled. . . .

Casanova's description of the carnival at Rome is fascinating: "For centuries Rome's Corso, during All Fools' Week, has been the most curious and entertaining thoroughfare in the world. The *barberi* gallop at full speed from the *Piazza del Popolo* down the Corso to the Column of Trajan, between two rows of carriages crowded against the far too narrow pavements, overflowing with masked and curious people of every walk of life. Every window is occupied. As soon as the *barberi* are past, the carriages proceed at a pace. The middle of the roadway teems with masked people afoot and on horseback. Confetti of sugar and plaster is tossed to and fro, as well as pamphlets and pasquinades. There is ceaseless banter. There is the greatest license throughout the crowd, composed of the lowest as well as the highest classes. At twenty-four hours, no sooner has the third cannon shot sounded from San Angelo, you would search the Corso in vain for a single mask or carriage. The crowd has poured into the adjoining streets, filling the theaters, the serious and the comic opera, etc. ...."

Here in Rome Casanova had occasion to move in the circles of the "men of the world." Among these the Englishman Lord Talon played a preeminent part. Casanova's memoirs tell us that he was an excellent violinist and that during his sojourn at Bonn he played a concerto by Tartini for the benefit of the Elector. As for Rome, all we hear is that Casanova was present at a shameless orgy led by Lord Talon.

In the *Teatro Aliberti* he heard a *castrato* who played the part of the primadonna: "His voice was magnificent, but even more magnificent was his beauty." Who this *castrato* was, I have been unable to learn, but it would appear that at the time he was turning all of Rome topsy-turvy. "One was madly in love before one even knew that one had felt anything. To resist him or to feel nothing would have meant that one was cold or prosaic, like a German. When he paced the stage waiting for the ritornel to his aria, his gait had something majestic and at once voluptuous. When he favored the boxes with glances from his eyes, their gentle and modest expression charmed and delighted every heart. Evidently he sought to nourish the love of those who loved him as a man and would probably not have loved him, had he been a woman. Holy Rome, which in this fashion forces all men to become pederasts, will not admit it and pretends not to believe in the effects of an illusion, much as it seeks to impress itself." This last sentence alludes to the Papal edict under which no woman could appear on the stage and as a result of which all feminine roles in the opera were sung by *castrati*. To Casanova, lover of women, such a prohibition must have seemed unacceptable in the extreme.

CHAPTER SIXTEEN

CASANOVA AS AN IMPRESARIO

FROM Rome Casanova went to Turin, where King Charles Emanuel III maintained an austere reign and where the adventurer, already notorious, was unable to obtain permission to stay. His funds were growing slim and so he was seized by an overwhelming passion for the Marquise d'Urfé. He hastened to Paris to stage the miracle of her rebirth as a man which the aged madwoman so fervently sought.

But here too the ground grew too hot under his feet. He went to Strassburg and thence to Augsburg where, in the summer of 1761, as plenipotentiary of the Portuguese Government, he participated in the peace negotiations. But the outrageous Casanova did little honor to the Government he was supposed to represent.

Here too the passion for the stage took hold of him. He met the aged Venetian theater director

Domenico Bassi, his childhood friend, who was having little success with his company. Casanova leased the theater and the entire personnel, taking the stage artists into his service at fifty florins a day. Any excess over this sum, if perchance found in the cashbox, was to be divided. Casanova sold the orchestra seats at high, the gallery seats at low prices —sometimes he even gave them away. The public thus slowly got into the habit of patronizing the theater. Despite these new interests Casanova did not neglect to pay major attention to the various actresses, but the adventures he had with them belong to another field!

From Augsburg Casanova traveled to Basle, and late in 1761 he again returned to Paris to carry to completion his great hoax with the Marquise. As we have already seen, he utilized the dancer Corticelli in this fraud, and she caused him no end of trouble. At a certain ball the "Countess Lascaris," as she was now styled, danced "in a fashion not permissible in a young girl of good background. She performed eightfold *entrechats, pirouettes, caprioles,* and *battements à mijambe*—in a word, all the tricks of an opera gamboler." Poor Casanova underwent tortures. Well, he soon got rid of his tormentor!

This adventure will preoccupy us again later on, but let us make mention now of the role played in it by Casanova's servant Gaetano Costa. For a long

125

time this man was Casanova's loyal assistant, a slave who helped him in the most daring exploits. It was he who acted the go-between in affairs of the heart, who functioned in the great hoaxes. He played a prominent part in the d'Urfé affair as well. Casanova entrusted to him the fortune of which he had bilked the Marquise. But the servant vanished with the money and Casanova was left empty-handed.

CHAPTER SEVENTEEN

ONCE AGAIN LA POMPEATI

WE may pass over the adventures of Casanova in Switzerland, Italy, and France, since they have little bearing on our subject. Let us accompany him to England, whither he now went, the Continent having become too hot for him. He took with him his adopted son, whom he had introduced to the Marquise by the false name of "Count Aranda," returning the lad to the arms of his mother, the erstwhile singer Teresa Pompeati, his old flame.

Count Aranda was a little mountebank on his own account. He could "play the flute, bestride a horse respectably, fence, and dance the minuet"—in short he had all the qualities of a *petit maître.*

In London the famous singer, whom Casanova had met in such reduced circumstances in the Netherlands, had become a "great lady" of somewhat questionable reputation. The former primadonna had married the Englishman Cornelys in the Netherlands. He had taken her to London, where at first she staged great concerts, later balls and festivities much frequented by the London citizenry and even the high peerage.

It is not quite easy today to form a picture of the social position of so ambiguous a creature as Mme. Cornelys. She had a luxuriously appointed house in London, as well as a countryseat. She had thirty-two servants, two secretaries, six horses, etc. Each year she staged twenty-four balls—twelve for the aristocracy, twelve for the commoners. Often as many as 500 or 600 persons took part. The admission charge was two guineas. It was accounted fashionable to show oneself at her gatherings. Even members of the royal family and the court frequented the home of this fabulous adventuress, who was reputed to have an annual income of 24,000 pounds sterling.

In his book, *England and Italy*, the historian Archenholtz (p. 206 ff) mistakenly describes Mme. Cornelys as a "German-Tyrolean" of low antecedents. "When she had made the acquaintance of aristocratic ladies," he writes, "she rented a very large and fine house and had it furnished in princely fashion. The entertainments she arranged there consisted of concerts, balls, and masquerades. Only subscribers were admitted and these had to present written authority from one of the presiding ladies.

Even then they were permitted to purchase no less than twelve tickets, initially at a cost of six guineas, later raised to nine. During the very first year she had as many as 2,700 subscribers. 'Founding Day' of the institution was celebrated each year by a masquerade to which everyone was admitted without distinction. Tickets were two guineas, but at two o'clock in the morning a magnificent nocturnal repast was served. I learned from her own lips that on more than one occasion 8,000 tickets were sold to such affairs. Not one of these occasions resembled any that had gone before. It was here that this woman's resourcefulness and genius were admirably displayed. There were illuminated colonnades and triumphal arches; halls transformed into gardens adorned with fountains and orange groves; labyrinthine flowerbeds; painted transparencies and inscriptions; stairways and lobbies heaped with colored lanterns in pyramid and other forms and festooned with garlands; dining tables arranged in horseshoe shape, offering a strange and beautiful spectacle; suites of rooms, each perfectly appointed in some Oriental style—Persian, Indian, Chinese. Yet all this variety was pervaded by a sense of order that only served to underscore the splendor. On 'Founding Day' some 9,000 wax tapers ordinarily burned in the various halls and rooms, and even these were arranged in many configurations to please the eye. Mme. Cornelys was never miserly.

On the contrary, she was always in debt, and after each ball had to go to prison. In the end the entertainments ceased and she who had been called the 'Empress of Good Taste' had to live on the charity of her friends."

In *Humphrey Clinker* by the English novelist Tobias Smollett, Lydia Melford writes a friend about the Cornelys entertainments. According to her letter she attended a party at Mme. Cornelys; the rooms, participants, costumes and decorations beggared description. But, she added, since she lacked the inclination for card-playing, she had failed to enter into the proper 'spirit' of the house.

When Casanova saw his old friend in London, she had her home on Soho Square. She received him in her luxurious palace like a perfect lady and not a familiar word was spoken, as though they knew each other merely "socially." Even little Sophie, the daughter who resembled Casanova in such revealing fashion that no one could be left in any doubt about her paternity, behaved in stiff and formal fashion toward him, at the behest of her mother. Sophie played and sang charmingly, to the piano and guitar. She danced a minuet with her brother, and afterward Casanova was permitted to dance another minuet with his daughter. He was himself an excellent dancer, and he executed it to perfection, to the delight of his little partner.

A few days later Casanova took part in one of the great balls. "The prodigality was worthy of a princely house.... Mme. Cornelys took in more than 1,200 guineas ... but her expenses were enormous." The consequences of her mismanagement were soon brought home. One day Casanova received a letter from his old friend, transmitted through his adopted son. It told him that she was in debtors' prison and asked him to stand bail. Casanova remained unmoved. He had not forgotten Teresa's poor behavior.

This was not the last time Mme. Cornelys was in debtors' prison. She was always short of cash, even in 1765, when she had arranged subscription concerts at which, among others, Johann Christian Bach, son of Johann Sebastian, officiated as conductor. Her star slowly faded, and the level of her entertainments rapidly declined. In the end she ran a public breakfast tavern. She died on August 19, 1797, aged seventy-four, in debtors' prison, under the commonplace name of Mrs. Smith. Truly, the prototype of the uproarious life of a singer in the eighteenth century!

Mme. Cornelys was not the only celebrity of the theater whom Casanova met in London. He also saw the dancer Binetti, whom he knew from Stuttgart and whom he later found again in Warsaw with her husband, the dancer Bic (or Pic). Both were at the time filling engagements at the Haymarket Theatre. Pic, by the way, played something of a part in the life of Mozart.

In Convent Garden Theatre Casanova listened to a certain singer named Sartori at a concert and also met the *castrato* singer Tenducci who, to Casanova's great surprise, introduced him to his wife by whom he had two children. "He laughed about the people," the adventurer relates, "who insisted that as a eunuch he was unable to beget progeny. Nature, he said, had created him a monster to preserve his manhood. He had been born a triorchis [a man with three testicles], and since the operation had removed but two testicles, the remaining one sufficed for the practice of his manhood."

Tenducci too played a part in the life of Mozart. In 1764, at the tender age of seven, Mozart came to London with his father—he arrived at the British capital shortly after Casanova's departure. It was Tenducci (and the *castrato* Giovanni Manzuoli) who gave young Mozart his first great impressions in the realm of song. Later on, in 1778, Mozart again met the *castrato*. This was in Paris, whither Mozart's friend Johann Christian Bach (who had business in Paris and had come to the French capital from London) had taken the singer. Mozart at the time wrote a "Scene" for Tenducci, which the singer took back to London, but it has been lost.

The *castrato*, so highly esteemed by the great

names in music and admired all over Europe, was later involved in a sensational divorce action. He had eloped with a Miss Dorothea Kinsman and lived with her for seven years during which she was not aware of his sexual impotency. But around 1784 Mme. Tenducci seems to have found a fly in the ointment. We have a letter from her to her father that reads: "The connubial relations that have taken place between me and my *castrato* can surely constitute no sacred bond in the eyes of the Almighty." The father at once sent her 200 guineas to free her from the hands of this "impotent monster." The daughter then started divorce proceedings.

"Tenducci," she deposed, "was born in Siena. He is now forty years old and when he was nine he was deprived of his manhood. He suffered complete castration by the Italian method, thereby becoming incapable of performing the sexual act and thus to consummate a marriage. Eight years ago Tenducci was introduced to the family of my father, an attorney in Dublin, in order to give me singing lessons. He found it not difficult to take advantage of my inexperience. We were secretly married with the aid of an old Catholic priest and made a secret escape. On arriving in Italy Tenducci said that I was a pupil entrusted to him by her parents. He was careful to avoid mention of a 'marriage,' since there is an Italian law that consigns a married *cas*-

trato to the gallows." The plaintiff concluded with the plea to have her marriage to Tenducci declared null and void and to make him liable for the costs. Her assertion that Tenducci was impotent, however, was untrue, for he later paid vigorous court to certain ladies in Paris.

The court, largely on the testimony of an Italian officer who had seen that Tenducci kept his testicles in a red velvet bag, annulled the marriage, especially in view of the fact that it had been solemnized by a Catholic priest (*Les Dessous de la pudibonderie anglaise*, II, 24 ff). Despite this scandal Tenducci continued his engagement at the Drury Lane Theatre until 1790. He died early in the nineteenth century in Italy.

CHAPTER EIGHTEEN

ADVENTURES IN RUSSIA

CASANOVA had to leave England precipitately on account of some trouble over a bank draft, and he now wanted to try his luck in Berlin. On the way he stopped over at Brunswick, where he was received at the court of the Hereditary Prince Charles William Ferdinand, members of which he knew from London. There he met the "munificent Signor Nicolini," director of the municipal and court theater. "He enjoyed the full favor of the generous prince," Casanova relates, "for his daughter Anna was the latter's mistress, and he lived rather luxuriously at Brunswick. He was an excellent theater manager. I accepted his invitation to dine at his table which was well worth my attention, both on account of the excellent cuisine and for the gracious company that assembled there every day. The guests were not distinguished by titles and decorations, but they lacked that servile and at once arrogant court manner that always bores me. . . . They were ladies and gentemen of talent and their gatherings made an exquisite picture."

Philippo Nicolini was in Brunswick from 1749 to 1771. His annual salary as theater director—and perhaps also for the complaisance with which he proferred his "pupils" to the Duke—came to 30,000 dollars. Lessing, at the very same time, drew about 300 dollars at court. In his time Nicolini was famous as the head of the *Compania dei piccoli Hollandesi*. This troupe of *Enfants Pantomimes,* consisting largely of Dutch children, was renowned all over Germany. Lessing called the *piccoli* "his little monkeys." In 1745 they were feted in Potsdam and Frankfurt, in 1746 in Munich, in 1747 in Vienna. There they gave a brilliant farewell performance before the Imperial Court and then went to Prague, where they remained until March 1748. Their forte was the splendid staging of their *intermezzi,* and their showpieces were Pergolesi's *Serva Padrona* and *Finto Pazzo,* Mariani's *Venetian Widow Drusilla* (Music by Sellitti), and Zanetti's *Li Birbi* (music by Fini). A young son of Felix Kurtz-Bernardon was a member of the company, which went to Hamburg in 1748 and the next year to Brunswick, where Nicolini continued to work until 1771 in the theater especially built for him.

Arrived in Berlin, Casanova paid his first visit to Raniero Calzabigi, brother of the Giovanni Calzabigi with whom Casanova had organized the first lottery in Paris in 1757. This younger brother too was a lottery expert. He had participated in the enterprise started by his brother and Casanova but, if we can believe Casanova, he had left Paris and his wife, the so-called "Lady General" La Motte, to establish a lottery at Brussels. Upon going into bankruptcy he presented himself to Frederic the Great of Prussia, who was always short of cash and who appointed him Court Councilor.

Young Calzabigi has a place in our merry-go-round, not because he was an adventurer and financial wizard, but because he entered into musical history as the great librettist for Gluck and a great reformer of the opera. At the time, in Berlin, he still had little connection with the theater, or at least we know little about it. His activities as a financier were all the more interesting.

Raniero Simone Francesco Calzabigi was born in Leghorn in 1714, the same year as Gluck (to whom he owes his immortality). His talent manifested itself at an early age—in two directions, as a poet and as a financier. In this respect he was of the same stripe as Casanova and Casanova's friend, the librettist Da Ponte. We meet him as a financier in Naples in 1743. Two years later, on the occasion of the marriage between the Dauphin of France and the daughter of Philip V of Spain, Maria Theresa, he wrote a pageant for which Manna composed the music. In 1747, on the occasion of the festivities attending the birth of an heir to the throne, Calzabigi was again called on as a court poet.

In Paris he became the assistant or partner of his brother Giovanni Antonio, who founded the lottery in Genoa. But the Paris lottery enterprise did not become successful until Casanova (who had come to Paris in 1757) joined the company. With the aid of his patron, Cardinal Bernis (in whose company he had once had those scandalous adventures with the nun M. M. at Venice), Casanova managed to gain entry to the Marquise de Pompadour and permission for establishing the lottery. Giovanni Calzabigi became its director, but Casanova preempted the finances for himself.

Now Casanova met young Calzabigi at Berlin. Through him the adventurer came to know a charming woman, Mme. Boulanger, Calzabigi's wife. Casanova spent almost every evening at the home of his fellow countryman, whose phenomenal luck as a lottery entrepreneur he never tired of praising. There he met another friend of his youth, the dancer Giovannina Denis, who was appearing in the ballet, dancing an exquisite solo. As a boy, when he was still a pupil of Dottore Gozzi, Casanova had fallen madly in love with the eight-year-old girl, then dancing a minuet at the theater. Little Giacomo, the great lover to be, had acually filched a sequin from his teacher in order to buy the girl a ring, for which she rewarded him with a kiss.

Now, twenty-seven years later, Casanova felt his old love for the now-famous ballerina reawaken. His intimate relationship with her lasted throughout his Berlin sojourn and was later renewed at Florence. She seems to have been endowed with uncommon physical charms. In Berlin she maintained an elegant salon, where Casanova met a number of dancers and musicians. He tells of the dancer Aubry, whom he knew from Paris, and whose fame rested on the fact that he had been the lover of one of the most highly placed ladies in Venice, while at the same time being her husband's favorite. It was said that the relationship was so intimate that Aubry slept beween the two spouses. At the close of the opera season the State Inquisitors had banished the dancer to Trieste. Aubry presented Casanova to his then wife, the dancer La Santina.

A fat gentleman also introduced himself to Casanova and claimed that he had known him for twenty-five years. He was the cellist Giuseppe da Loglio, a member of the Imperial Russian Orchestra from 1735 to 1764. In Warsaw Da Loglio had been entrusted with a diplomatic mission to the Republic of Venice, whither he went in 1756 to die there six years later. He was married to the daughter of the famous violinist Lodovico Madonis, whose first name Casanova wrongly gives as Giovanni.

(Madonis was born late in the seventeenth century in Venice, where Frederic the Great's flautist, Quantz, heard him. In 1729 he appeared in the *Concerts Spirituels* at Paris. In 1731 he was called to St. Petersburg as concert master, and he remained there until 1767. His violin works are preserved in the Library at Leningrad.)

Discussing his sojourn at Berlin further, Casanova tells us that the shutters of the room in which he lived at the inn were always closed, because the dancer Reggiana had once lived there and had accidentally been spied by the passing King in a state of nature. The King was in love with the famous dancer Barberina (Barbara de Campanini), but she had treated him harshly. He was afraid he might suffer the same fate with Reggiana, and hence curtly ordered that the shutters be kept closed.

When Casanova came to St. Petersburg to try his luck there, he presented a letter of recommendation from La Santina to the beautiful dancer Mecour. Another letter of recommendation from the hand of Da Loglio got him a very friendly reception on the part of the *castrato* Luini, lover of the primadonna, Mme. Colonna. "They seemed to be together only to torment each other, for I did not see them in accord a single day." At Luini's house Casanova met the famous *castrato* Millico, who esteemed him highly. Millico later was the teacher of Gluck's niece who, according to Burney's report of 1772, "had so well absorbed Millico's taste and expression."

In St. Petersburg Casanova met another old friend, the Venetian Roccolini who "had left Venice on a whim to sing at the St. Petersburg Opera, though she knew not a note and had never been on the stage before." Unable to obtain a theatrical engagement at St. Petersburg, she was trying her hand at procuring.

Casanova dined at Locatelli's, run by the former Prague theater director, by imperial privilege, at the "Red Tavern" in the *Katherinenhof.* He was in the company of the leading beauty of St. Petersburg, Proté. Whether Locatelli's wife, the former Prague diva Giovanna della Stella, was with him in St. Petersburg Casanova does not tell us.

Returning from St. Petersburg, Casanova stopped over in Kaporie to rest. "Two days later we met the famous orchestra conductor Galuppi, called *Il Buranello,* who was on the way to St. Petersburg with two friends and a virtuosa. He knew me and was very much surprised to find an excellent meal in the Venetian style at the inn where he was stopping and to be received by a gentleman with a compliment in his mother tongue. As soon as I told him my name, he embraced me with cries of surprise and satisfaction."

Let us on this occasion reproduce a remark by Catherine II, cited by Casanova. One night, as the Empress was leaving the Opera, where Metastasio's *Olympias* had been given (probably to Galuppi's music—Casanova mentions only the librettist), she said: "This opera music seems to have entertained everyone. Therefore I am delighted with it, though it bored me. Music is something fine, but I don't understand how one can love it passionately—at least not when one has something important to do or to think about. I am now going to send for *Il Buranello* [Galuppi]. I am curious if he will be able to make the music appear interesting to me, but I doubt it. . . ."

At the time, in 1765, Galuppi was coming to St. Petersburg for the second time, remaining there for three years.

CHAPTER NINETEEN

POLISH INTERLUDE; SOJOURN IN AUSTRIA AND GERMANY

IN Poland there occurred a dangerous interlude in the comedy of Casanova's life. There the jealousy of two dancers embroiled our hero in a duel with a Polish aristocrat, Branicki. The reader will recall the dancer Binetti whom Casanova had met in Stuttgart and later in London. In Stuttgart she had kept him out of jail, but in Warsaw she nearly cost him his life. It happened because the dancer Catai, wife of the Warsaw theater director Tomatis, feared that Binetti might dispute her preeminence.

The Polish King, Stanislaus Augustus, shunned no expense to attract the leading capacities in the opera, drama, and ballet to his stage. He had expressed a desire to see Binetti dance. Indeed, he had posted 1,000 ducats for the purpose, and Casanova was happy to bring the good news to the dancer. Within three days Pic, Binetti's partner, had arranged a ballet, and so great was her success that within scarcely twelve days she had an exquisitely appointed house, a cellar full of choice wines, and numerous admirers.

The audience was divided into two camps. One swore by the fair Catai, the other by the graceful and talented Binetti who, despite her artistry, was permitted to dance only in the "second ballet." She invoked the support of the Crown Chamberlain Branicki, the most influential man in Poland, but bitterly hated for his brutality. Casanova loved and esteemed Binetti, but this time he was on the side of Catai, with whose husband he had become very friendly. The Pole picked a public quarrel and its result was the duel, sensationally reported throughout the European press. Casanova was shot in the wrist, Branicki in the abdomen. Our hero was in grave danger of being sentenced to death, and only his popularity at court saved him. But the happy days in Poland were over, and in company of Count Clary from Teplitz in Bohemia Casanova traveled to Breslau.

Meanwhile we hear more theater gossip. Binetti's good fortune in Poland did not last long. "Binetti's husband ran away with his wife's chambermaid, taking along diamonds, jewelry, linens, and even the silverware. He left her to his *Mignon*, the dancer Pic." It should be noted that the term *Mignon* then denoted a homosexual "friend."

By the way of Dresden, where he found his

mother, Casanova went to Vienna, making a brief stop-over in Prague. He arrived in Vienna late in 1767. On New Year's Day 1768 he visited the two librettists Metastasio and Calzabigi, whom he had last met in Berlin. In Brussels Calzabigi had made the acquaintance of the Austrian politician Count Cobenzl, who had brought him to Vienna. There Calzabigi came forward with commercial and financial plans, such as a project for founding a bank in Vienna, Prague, Milan, and Brussels. He gained the favor of the all-powerful Chancellor Kaunitz, a passionate admirer of the French theater, and he succeeded in having Count Durazzo, who shared his own taste in everything, called to Vienna in 1754 to direct the theater of Vienna.

At the time there were two camps in Vienna (as later in Paris with the Gluckists and the Piccinists) —on the one side Metastasio and Hasse, on the other Calzabigi and Gluck. It is easily seen where Casanova stood, when we read: "This Calzabigi, whose whole body was covered with boils, almost always worked in bed, which he scarcely ever left. The Minister visited him almost every day. I was often with Metastasio and went to the theater every day, where Vestris, whom the young Emperor had sent for from Paris, danced. I . . . attended the theater regularly and often dined with Calzabigi, who boasted of his atheism and reviled Metastasio in the most brazen fashion. Metastasio, on his part, merely held Calzabigi in contempt. Calzabigi knew this, but merely laughed about it. He was a great political schemer and the right hand of Prince Kaunitz."

On the subject of Vestris the diary of Prince Khevenhüller-Metsch says under date of January 11, 1767: "In the evening there was the first appearance at the *Burgtheater* of the famous dancer Vestris, a native Italian who had once lived here with his parents and brothers and sisters in Sellier's time, dancing on the very same stage as a boy. Later he had become first dancer at the Paris Opera, where he had acquired a great reputation in his art. He had accepted an engagement at Stuttgart for this carnival. But the Duke of Württemberg, because of his well-known peccadilloes, had agreed with his subjects to undertake great reforms in his household, himself retiring to Venice for a while. Thus M. Vestris, to keep from remaining idle, sought an opportunity to display his artistry here or in Warsaw."

As was to be expected, Casanova came into conflict with the notorious Vienna Chastity Commission, created under the aegis of the austere Empress Maria Theresa and the terror of all libertines. It has left its last literary traces in the *Rosenkavalier* by Hofmannsthal and Strauss. Casanova was expelled from Vienna and went to Stuttgart by way of Linz and Augsburg. There he met his old friend Balletti, the dancer Toscani (Sittard, II, 45, men-

146

tions an *"artificier"* *Toscani* who may have been the dancer's husband) "who was the Duke's mistress, and Vestris." It is noteworthy that we now find Vestris in Stuttgart, though at the beginning of the year he had been in Vienna. A diary passage of Prince Khevenhüller of September 10, 1767, tells us that on that date a ballet, *L'Apotheose d'Hercule*, had been performed in Vienna, *"de la composition du fameux Sr. Noverri de Hongard* . . . while yesterday M. Vestris, by special permission of the King, returned from Paris for the present season."

Hence Casanova undoubtedly met the famous dancer at Stuttgart on the latter's trip from Paris to Vienna—unless he had a lapse of memory. The adventurer paid court to Vestris' wife, "a beautiful actress" who had but one fault, her inability to pronounce the letter "r." Greatly pleased with the young actress, Casanova explained that this medicine chest held an infallible cure for her affliction. "You may slap my face," he told her, "if I don't have a part for you by tomorrow which you will be able to read without revealing your fault. If, on the other hand, you do read it as your husband, for example, would do, then you shall permit me to give you a tender kiss."

Casanova actually sat down and overnight wrote (or rather rewrote) a play in such a way that the part for the young actress contained not a single "r." . . . The girl was Anna Friederike Heinel

(1752-1808), at the time sixteen years old, a pupil of Noverre, according to one tradition the inventor of the pirouette.

From Stuttgart Casanova went to Mannheim, to the Palatine court. In Schwetzingen he met the court poet Veraci. "Of all the poets I know Veraci is the most curious. To distinguish himself from other poets he has chosen a style that is the precise opposite of that of the great Metastasio. He uses only masculine rhymes and insists that his verses are easier to set to music for a composer. Jomelli seems to have given him this strange notion."

Mateo Veraci or Verazi played a certain part in Jomelli's life. He had been court poet at Mannheim since 1756, and at the same time Italian private secretary to the Elector. He wrote a large number of librettos that were set to music by Jomelli at Stuttgart, and also by Anfossi and others. Abert says of them that they closely follow Metastasio in the main, though without achieving the latter's grace and nobility. Jomelli occasionally had to correct the texts himself. Writing about Jomelli, the poet Schubart says: "He studied his poet, often correcting him, which was often necessary especially with Verazi."

Verazi was a close friend of Jomelli's who had him called to Ludwigsburg from Schwetzingen in the fall of 1769. In a letter to Duke Charles Eugene Verazi reported that he had material for two dramatic works, *The Death of Socrates* and *Orpheus*. Jomelli later fell into disfavor and left Württemberg. He wrote to Veraci from Aversa in 1770, requesting his old friend to settle his affairs. But Veraci, to whom Jomelli owed money, satisfied his claim from the composer's effects. This trait of the librettist fits in well with Casanova's report "that he never again saw the property he had left with Veraci. . . ."

CHAPTER TWENTY

SPAIN

THE quest for happiness, for more adventure, for true love which he was never able to find, drove Casanova on. He had long wanted to try his luck in Spain and Portugal. The fair Portuguese Pauline in London had made such a deep impression on him that he contemplated following her to her homeland. On the way, as was to be expected, he stopped over in Paris, where he arrived in October 1767. He attended a concert opposite the blind alley of the *Orangerie*. There he met the Marquis de Lille, nephew of the Marquise d'Urfé, meanwhile deceased. The Marquis insultingly reproached him with having bilked his aunt of at least a million. There was a public quarrel, as a result of which Casanova was expelled from Paris.

The road now led to Spain, by way of Orleans and Bordeaux. In Orleans too Casanova met old friends. The Bodin-Geoffrois had settled there, the

PLATE 11.
Carlo Broschi Detto Farinelli, Famous Italian Castrato

PLATE 12.
Mozart-Keller in Prague's Tempelgässchen, the Tavern Where
Mozart Used to Meet His Friends

dancer couple Casanova had originally met in Vienna in 1754. "I had myself conducted to Bodin," Casanova relates, "once a fine dancer who had married La Geoffroi—one of my thousand mistresses whom I first knew twenty-two years ago. I had later met her in Turin, Vienna and Paris. . . . Such a surprise, such scenes of reunion, such a reviving of old memories, old pleasures! This has always been my weak, or perhaps my strong side. For a moment I thought I was again what I had once been, and my soul rejoiced in telling my experiences or listening to theirs. I took pleasure in them, because my conscience was tormented by no regrets. Bodin's wife had grown ugly rather than old. To please her husband, she had become devout to boot, giving God what the Devil had left her. Bodin lived on the proceeds of a small estate he had bought and ascribed to the avenging justice of God all the misfortunes that befell this estate in the course of the years. We dined frugally for it was Friday and the precepts of the Church were inviolable. I told him at leisure of my experiences since the time we had last met, and when I was done we mused at length over the changing fortunes of men's lives, when they fail to permit religion to guide them in all things. My host told me what I knew equally well, or perhaps even better—namely that there is a God, that I had a soul and that it was high time for me to follow their example and renounce the vanities of the world."

It must have been edifying to see the old sinner Geoffroi, once so much given to amorous dalliance, calling the attention of her erstwhile lover, the arch-reprobate Casanova, to the adventages of heavenly bliss. . . . But Casanova was not yet ripe for them. He hastened toward new adventures.

He met with little luck in Madrid. A passionate dancer, he soon learned how to dance the *fandango*. Here too he attended the Italian Opera, of which he tells us something. His skill as an occasional librettist stood him in good stead in Madrid: "An Italian conductor wanted to have a new play to set to music. . . . The time was too short to send to Italy, and so I declared myself ready to compose a play on the spot. I was taken by my word and turned over the first act to him the next day. The maestro put it to music within four days' time, and the Venetian Ambassador invited all the musicians to attend the rehearsal of this act in the great hall of his palace. The two remaining acts had likewise been written by this time. The music was highly praised and in a fortnight the whole opera was produced. . . . In the process of writing the opera I had come to know the artists. The leading one was a Roman woman named Pellicia."

Casanova praises her beauty, her "squinting eyes," and obtained for her recommendations to Valencia, whither she went with the opera director Marescalchi, there to perform Italian opera for the first time. According to Casanova, Pellicia later married a famous violinist who had been engaged at the Italian Opera at the same time. Casanova tells that she conceived verses to Roman melodies, which she recited with extraordinary grace. In Valencia the same operas were played as at Madrid. But *opera buffa* was still considered too risky. "The Inquisition had its satanic eyes open far too wide." I have been unable to establish who Marescalchi was. Perhaps he is identical with Luigi Marescalchi, listed by Gerber and Fétis, a student of P. Martini who lived in Venice in 1770 and kept a musical shop there and in Naples. But the Library of Congress has a whole series of operatic texts by Marescalchi.

Casanova had only unpleasant experiences in Spain. Because of a crude indiscretion, he quarreled with the Venetian Ambassador Manucci. In Barcelona he had the audacity to dally with a dancer named Nina, friend of the Governor General of Catalonia, Count Ricla. This was bound to lead to trouble.

Casanova describes the "coarse habits" of Nina in his characteristic manner. She had once been the wife of the dancer Bergonzi, and her father had been the famous *Ciarlatano* Pelandi. Count Ricla was so jealous that he charged the Bolognese singer Molinari with watching over her. The dancer's own story is a little romance in itself, later told to

Casanova by Nina's sister. Nina must indeed have
been something of a monster. Casanova explains
her character by the fact that she was supposed to
have been the offspring of an incestuous relationship between her sister and her father, Pelandi, the
Ciarlatano, who must have been a monster himself.
By all accounts Nina was a "vamp" of the worst
kind. As a dancer her main attraction was the *rebaltade*, a kind of back flip with pirouettes.

At her first appearance there was thunderous applause in the pit because, during the *rebaltade*,
Nina had exposed her drawers to the belt. Now in
Spain there was a law under which any dancer who
exposed her drawers to the public on the stage was
fined one dollar. When she was so advised by the
Inspector, Nina simply danced the *rebaltade* the
next day without wearing any drawers at all—thus
technically staying within the law. The audience
went mad, partly from indignation, partly from enthusiasm. As for the Governor of Catalonia, he
went quite out of his mind, and the shameless courtesan was henceforth able to do with him as she
pleased.

After Casanova had played some uproarious
pranks with her, the jealous Count Ricla plotted an
attempt on his life. When it failed, the Count had
Casanova arrested on some trifling pretext. Casanova spent a full forty-two days incarcerated in the
Citadel and there wrote a historical work, *A Refu-*

tation of the "History of Venice" by Amelot. Its purpose was to get its author back into the good graces of the Venetian State Inquisitors. An authority on Casanova, Viktor Ottmann, states that this book, written in prison without any reference facilities, does the greatest honor to its author's knowledge of history.

But let us follow Casanova's "artistic" career further. A journey from Spain to Italy was now on his program, and on the way, in a chateau in southern France, he met Henriette, the excellent cellist he had once so adored. She was now a wealthy widow and she offered to help Casanova. Unfortunately he tells us nothing of her artistic career.

CHAPTER TWENTY-ONE

FARINELLI, THE CASTRATO

IN the years 1770/71 Casanova was again in Italy, In Rome he frequented the Aliberti, Capronica, and Torrenona Theatres, and among the celebrities of Rome he mentions in this connection is the famous singer Gabrielli, nicknamed *Cuochetta*, then zealously courted by Prince Borghese. She carried the name *Cuochetta* because she was the daughter of Prince Gabrielli's cook. The Prince, overhearing her sing at work, had her trained first by Garcia, then by Porpora. In 1750, twenty years old, she had come to Naples where Metastasio heard her and brought her to Vienna. There she became the favorite singer of Francis I. She visited Russia and Sicily. In Parma the Infante Don Philip was her lover. She died at Rome in 1796, a wealthy woman.

Casanova met another famous singer in Florence. She was Maddalena Allegranti, with whose uncle, the innkeeper G. B. Allegranti, Casanova took lodgings. He was then no longer a young man, while Maddalena—so the adventurer tells us—was still almost a child and so charming, graceful, and clever that she seriously distracted him from his studies. She would occasionally come to his room, wish him a pleasant day, and inquire how he had spent the night. "The sight of her, the sound of her voice ... I could not resist. ... I was afraid she might seduce me and did not wish to seduce her. I could think of no way out except to take flight. ... A few years later Maddalena became a famous singer." Allegranti was later a pupil of the composer Holzbauer. In 1771 she appeared on the stage in Venice. From 1774 on she was in Mannheim, and after some interludes in Italy she went to England in 1781. Her life story is obscure.

In Florence Casanova renewed another old acquaintance, with the dancer Denis whom he had met in Berlin. She was his own age and, as he says, "of a charming freshness. She had the gracious nature of a young girl, was very graceful and was in command of the customs of good society. She dressed exquisitely. In addition, she had a lovely apartment on the main square, one flight up over the most popular coffee-house in Florence." As was to be expected, Casanova was soon on the most intimate terms with the charming lady.

Of greater interest from the viewpoint of musical history is Casanova's encounter with the *castrato*

Farinelli whom he visited late in May 1771. He reports: "The Elector of Saxony's dowager came to
Bologna, and I hastened to pay her my respects.
The princess had come for the sole reason of visiting the famous *castrato* Farinelli who had left the
court of Spain to spend his life in wealth and ease
at Bologna. He gave a splendid breakfast for the
princess and sang an aria he had composed himself,
to his own piano accompaniment. The dowager, a
passionate music lover, embraced the *castrato* and
exclaimed: 'Now I can die in peace.'

"Farinelli, called Chevalier Don Carlo Broschi,
had himself reigned in Spain, as it were. But Queen
Elizabeth of Parma, Philip V's consort, had hatched
intrigues that caused Broschi to leave the court.

"Looking at a portrait of the Queen, presented
in full figure by Amigoni, the dowager said a few
words in her praise, mentioning an incident that
had happened under the reign of Ferdinand VI.
The magnificent singer broke into tears which he
vainly sought to restrain.

"Broschi may have been about seventy years old
when I saw him in Bologna. He was very rich, enjoyed excellent health, yet was nevertheless unhappy, for he had nothing to do and always tearfully
yearned for his beloved Spain. . . . He had a nephew
who was to inherit all his wealth. He married this
nephew to a high-born lady from Tuscany and was
happy in anticipation of the aristocratic family that

158

bade fair to spring from his line, though but in the second generation. Yet this marriage, instead of making him happy, only caused him torment. For despite his advanced age and his impotency he unhappily fell in love with his niece and grew jealous of his nephew. To fill the cup of his wretchedness, he was an object of loathing to his beloved. . . ."

In a letter dated June 14, 1772, from Bologna to Prince Casimir Lubomirski, Casanova speaks of Farinelli: "The Elector's dowager has passed through here coming from Rome. In the evening she was entertained by the Cardinal Legate and in the morning she visited the famous *castrato* Farinelli. She spent two hours with him and sang with him. . . ."

Farinello or Farinelli, whose true name was Carlo Broschi (Farinelli was the name of an uncle which he assumed), was born on January 24, 1705, at Andria in Apulia. Allegedly he had been castrated at a very tender age on account of an injury he suffered in an unfortunate fall. This "injury," however, was merely a legend put forward in protection against the law prohibiting castration and against evil tongues. Actually his castration—as in most other cases of the unsexing of singers—was due to the unbridled avarice of his parents who were exploiting the boy's fine voice. Carlos studied with the famous singing teacher Nicola Porpora, and the young singer soon appeared in Rome and in other Italian cities with great success. Many anecdotes circulated about his life and his fabulous success. From 1734 to 1737 he was in England, whither Porpora, then engaged at Lincoln's and Innfield's Theatres and embroiled in keen rivalry with Handel, had called him.

Burney tells of the phenomenal effect exerted by Farinelli's artistry. The first rehearsal took place in the house of the primadonna Cuzzoni. When Farinelli began to sing, Lord Cooper, Principal Manager of the Opera, remarked that the four accompanying musicians, all of them capable artists, were not following the singer but simply staring at him thunderstruck. Lord Cooper requested them to pay closer attention. The musicians then confessed themselves unable to keep pace with Farinelli, overwhelmed as they were by amazement at Farinelli's talent. All of London was in the grip of enthusiasm for Farinelli. Innumerable cartoons, newspaper reports, satires, memoirs, and letters tell us of Farinelli's unheard-of successes. In 1736 he went to Spain by way of France, and in Spain he succeeded, by means of his singing to restore the melancholic Philip V to participation in the affairs of the world and of government.

There was but one thing that stirred the brooding king—music. This is what Giovanni Sacchi, Farinelli's biographer (*Vita del Cavaliere Don Carlo Broschi*, 1784), writes about the singer's arrival in

Madrid: "Farinelli arrived on August 7, 1737. Queen Elizabeth arranged a concert in a hall close to the King's own apartment. She asked Farinelli to recite a few of his most engaging songs. King Philip at first seemed surprised, then deeply moved. After the second aria, he summoned the singer to his chambers, overwhelmed him with compliments and asked for a third piece, in which Farinelli surpassed himself. Carried away, the King asked him what reward he wanted. Nothing would be denied him. Farinelli asked that the King allow himself to be shaved and dressed, that he rise from his depression and again appear in the Council of State."

The King was actually persuaded to comply with these requests, and from this moment on his affliction improved. The credit was attributed to Farinelli, and efforts were made to keep him at the court at any cost. Although jealous courtiers accused him of sorcery, he was appointed for life, at a salary which, according to Sacchi, equaled his London income, put by Burney at more than 3,000 pounds sterling. To this were added a house, a team of horses from the King's stables and caparisoned in the King's livery, etc. This position as a favorite was made dependent on the obligation to sing exclusively for the King. Hence Farinelli's voice, at the time of his prime, was lost to his contemporaries. Farinelli became the King's friend and constant counselor. Every day he had to sing four arias for the King, and legend has it that for ten full years they were always the same four arias. . . ."

In the National Library at Vienna there is a luxuriously bound collection of arias, with a dedication by Farinelli to the Austrian Empress Maria Theresa. It is one of these arias from Giacomelli's opera *Merope*—an aria entitled *Quell'usignuolo,* in which the singer is called on to imitate the nightingale's song in artful variations—that is supposed to have particularly pleased the melancholic King.

Philip V died in 1746 and his successor, Ferdinand VI, likewise afflicted with a hereditary taint, followed in his footsteps. Farinelli's position at court remained unchanged, except that he enjoyed even greater liberties. He was now permitted to sing in public at court and celebrated his greatest triumphs before the court dignitaries. It is not true that Farinelli was actually Prime Minister, but he did carry the greatest weight at court and with the King.

Ferdinand's successor, Charles III, was more active and coarse-fibered than his predecessors. He dismissed Farinelli at once, and when a pleader called attention to the singer's merits and good qualities, the King merely said cynically: "All well and good, but capons are good only for eating." Thus Farinelli left the Spanish court and in 1761 settled permanently in Bologna. He was a world celebrity. No wonder every distinguished visitor to Italy was eager to visit him—including Casanova.

Burney visited Farinelli in 1770. He had come to Bologna only on account of Padre Martini and Farinelli. He relates that Farinelli had long since stopped singing, though he was still amusing himself on the grand piano and the viola d'amour. . . . Burney supplies a comprehensive biography of the famous singer, including data on his sojourn in Spain where Farinelli had to sing the same four arias for Philip V every evening, two of them set by Hasse. Burney also mentions Farinelli's yearning for Spain: "He seems very much to regret the being obliged to seek a new habitation, after having lived twenty-four years in Spain, where he had formed many friendships and connections that were dear to him."

Count Lamberg, in his *Mémorial d'un Mondain*, also tells of Farinelli, in whose villa, just outside Bologna, he was magnificently received. Farinelli had the most perfectly courtly manners. When the Queen of Spain was mentioned, he exhibited a portrait—the one by Amigoni, described by Casanova as well—and exclaimed: "It is she who enabled me to give my niece a seemly dowry. I married her off, and six times a day she puts her hand under my chin, lest I withdraw my favor from her. I desire her to visit a watering place to make up for my infirmity, in order that my nephews may gain by her children."

Farinelli was just having his portrait painted, in order to send the picture to Prince Kaunitz. He loved to talk about people, kings and courts. "Look at this clavicembalo. It is of quite ordinary wood, yet all of Europe believes that I carried it away from Spain, studded with diamonds." He had several favorite instruments and distinguished them by the names of the most famous painters. He trilled an aria by Galuppi on his "Raphael." His rooms were adorned with portraits of the great. His own likeness, in the uniform of the Order of Calatrava, painted by Amigoni, hung beside those of Metastasio, Faustina (Bordoni), and the painter himself. Pointing to his *alter ego,* he said: "This is C. [Coglione] di Broschi, of whom Prospero—the great Prospero Lambertini [Benedict XIV]—said: 'He left behind in Italy what he found again in Spain. C . . c honori.' " He had a son in the Spanish service in India and once said, in the deepest confidence: "I do not regret that I have aged. But I should like to have back what I lost in Italy." A young woman asked him what that was. He replied: "One of my eyes."

In 1767 the French writer Duclos, on the way home from Italy to Paris, stopped over in Bologna. He too visited Farinelli. Although he had once had a liaison with Camargo, he was given to a moralizing tone. But in the end his report is much like those of other witnesses.

Keyssler too expands on Farinelli and his famous colleagues: "Among the singers of Italy today no one disputes first place to Carlo Broschi detto Farinelli, both in singing technique and in beauty of voice. His range is twenty-three full tones, without falsetto. No one remembers ever having heard anything like it and it is said to be a gift bestowed by the Holy Virgin in return for the great devotion shown by Farinelli's mother. He is but twenty-two years old and likely to achieve much in his art.

"After him, among the singers of Italy, Giovanni Carestini deserves next place because of his sonorous and powerful voice, and then come Senesino, Giacanto Fontana detto Farfarello, Gaetano Majorano detto Caffarello, Angelo Amerovoli, Nicolini, Gaetano Valfetta di Milano, etc.—all of them men whom nature has denied the adornment of a beard. This lack, together with the clear, feminine voices, at first makes it appear strange for smooth-faced singers to appear on the stage in the guise of blood-thirsty warriors urging on their men to deeds of valor. But the opera is no place for the exercise of such acute judgment. It is the ears that are to be tickled. Hence one seeks neither verisimilitude in the intrigues of such spectacles, nor skilled and poetic expression of thought. It is the music of the arias that is composed rather than the text, and the author of the latter is often compelled to insert syllables with the vowels 'e' and 'a,' regardless of meaning, because these are the sounds with which a skilled throat can best display its runs and trills. The Italian tongue has the advantage over other languages in that even its nouns are full of vowels that are easy to sing."

Arteaga, finally, in its history of Italian opera (German translation by Forkel, 1789), speaks of Farinelli: "In our time no one else has been endowed by nature with such excellent, powerful, and at once flexible tones. No other voice was as well-tempered and voluminous. It embraced all tones without distinction, no matter how high or deep. A creative imagination, coupled with vocal flexibility over the entire range, enabled him to contrive a thousand new and strange forms of song. . . . The purest intonation to which his art adhered as though to the canons of Polycletus, an extraordinary ease, an unheard-of skill in trills, an agreeable moderation in the embellishments, an equal skill in the light and the pathetic styles, a slow crescendo and diminuendo of the voice over the entire range as required by the interpretation—these are the admirable virtues he was generally conceded to possess, enabling him to attain that great good fortune known to everyone."

Because of its famous singing academy, Bologna became the starting point for almost all Italian singers. Casanova expressed himself about the school in not very respectful tones: "During Lent I made the acquaintance of some very charming singers and dancers at Bologna. Bologna is the nursery of this tribe, and all these theatrical heroines are quite reasonable and easy to obtain, so long as they are in their very own country." It was in Bologna too that Casanova met the dancer Nina Bergonzi, a shameless courtesan whose acquaintance he had made in Spain, La Marcucci whom he also knew from Spain, and La Soavi whom he had met in Parma and who later played a part in the Paris and Venice Operas. He visited the famous and wealthy dancer Sabbatini as well.

CHAPTER TWENTY-TWO

CASANOVA AGES

CASANOVA'S memoirs break off with the year
1774. We know about the remainder of his
life in part from the Venetian state archives, in part
from the archives of Count Waldstein at Dux in
Bohemia, transferred to Hirschberg in Bohemia
after the First World War.

After long peregrinations through Europe, Casanova landed in his native city of Venice on September 3, 1774. It was eighteen years since the Inquisition there had arrested him and thrown him into
the Leads, whence he had made his famous escape.
The conditions under which he now had to arrange
his life were not edifying. He was compelled to sup-
ply the Inquisition with secret reports on certain
personages and circles—in other words, he became
a spy. He lived in Venice for some years, in retire-

ment and in circumstances that were by no means magnificent.

But Casanova was destined to continue his adventurous career. He was one of those men for whom there is no peace on earth. There was a quarrel with his old patron, the patrician Grimani, at the latter's house. Casanova, that old knight of the pen, was unable to resist composing a polemic against Grimani under the title *Ne Amori ne Donne overo la Stalla d'Augia repulita.* The upshot of this headlong action was another and irrevocable edict of banishment. He left his native city in September 1782, went to Trieste and Vienna, then sojourned in several cities of Upper Italy, later in Augsburg, Frankfurt, Cologne, Aachen, Amsterdam, etc., finally returning to Paris in 1784. He was disillusioned, tired, depressed. He was fifty-eight years old. His restless life had been without a proper profession, and the ailments brought on by a thousand and one dissipations and vices had left their mark on him.

He looked forward to the day when he might retire to some corner to live on the charity of some compassionate soul. When he was flush he had been prodigal and generous toward others, but he had put nothing aside. In the spring of 1784 or 1785, as fate would have it, he came upon Count Joseph von Waldstein, manorial lord of Dux and Oberleutensdorf in Bohemia. Waldstein was one of the most highly placed aristocrats of Bohemia, a descendant of the famed generalissimo of the Thirty Years' War.

Casanova met the Count at the Venetian Embassy, being introduced by his friend, *Abbé* Eusebio della Lena. The incident is described by the witty Prince de Ligne, uncle of the Count, who was in the party. Waldstein pretended to believe in magic and to be preoccupied with the subject. He spoke of the "Key of Solomon," of Agrippa, and of other matters in the field of magic.

"To whom are you telling this?" Casanova exclaimed. "Oh! *Che bella cosa! Cospetto!*"

"I am interested in all these things," Waldstein replied. "Why don't you come with me to Bohemia? I am leaving tomorrow."

But the spoiled adventurer did not immediately accept the invitation. He first accompanied his brother Francesco, the painter of battle scenes, to Vienna where he became secretary to the Venetian Ambassador Foscarini. When Foscarini died, Casanova, deserted by all his friends and penniless, resumed his pilgrimage, headed for Berlin, where he hoped to receive an appointment. On the way he stopped in Brno, visiting his friend, Count Maximilian Lamberg. He then went on to Czaslau in Bohemia, where he made the acquaintance of the German-Bohemian author J. F. Opitz. From Czaslau he went to Karlsbad by way of Prague. Thence he went to Teplitz and it was here that he again ran into Count Waldstein. Waldstein took him along to Castle Dux which is but a few miles from Teplitz. Henceforth Casanova remained Waldstein's librarian at Dux, a tiny provincial town in Bohemia, far from the beaten path and the affairs of the world. His post was a sinecure created by his generous master, who did all he could to make the old adventurer's declining years as pleasant as possible. Casanova had servant and carriage and even a cook to prepare his favorite dishes.

When his master was in residence everything went well. He ate at the Count's table, and the Count even encouraged his literary activities. But Casanova was like a caged lion. He who thought he had a monopoly on the pleasures of the world now felt himself to be a servant, a prisoner. He wrote and wrote ceaselessly—letters, his memoirs, brief plays (such as *Polemoscope*) meant for the amateur stage, and a utopian novel, *Icosameron*. He often made trips to Teplitz, Oberleutensdorf, and even Prague. On one occasion he fled to Berlin. He never got further than that in the fourteen years of his voluntary exile.

He gradually turned into an ill-tempered, irritable old man who vented his displeasure over every petty injury. When the Count was absent, Casanova was consigned to the dinner company of the Castle Steward Feltkirchner, a coarse individual, to whom he wrote sarcastic, devastating letters, though whether his adversary ever read them is a matter of doubt.

The sharpest picture of Casanova in his old age is given by Prince de Ligne in his *Fragment on Casanova*. He states there that "for six summers I have had the pleasure of enjoying conversations with Casanova, seasoned with the imagination of a twenty-year-old youth, warm friendship, and rich and useful learning."

It is interesting to note how Casanova's character revealed itself in his old age. He had changed in many ways, but at bottom he was the same man. Of course the witty Prince's predilection for exaggeration must be taken into account. "Not a day passed," the Prince relates, "that he did not create an uproar throughout the house over his coffee, his milk, or the plate of macaroni he demanded every day. Now it was the cook who had put too much salt in his *polenta*, now the stablemaster who had assigned him so wretched a coachman that he was ashamed to go driving, now the dogs whose barking had robbed him of his sleep. On account of guests expected by Count Waldstein, he had been compelled to dine alone at a small table; or a hunting horn had assailed his ears early in the morning with its piercing false notes. The local minister drew his ire by efforts to convert him, or the Count had failed to bid him 'Good morning.' . . . His soup had been maliciously served too hot or the servant had kept him waiting before serving the wine. He would complain of not having been presented to some celebrity who had come to Dux to see the lance with which the great Waldstein had been murdered, and there were other grievances. He had been denied access to the arsenal, from pure malice and not because the key was lost. The Count had lent out a book without giving him notice. Again, one of the grooms had failed to doff his hat or had spoken German which he could not understand. Or there had been laughter over his anger, or he had shown his French verses and again there had been laughter. He had recited his Italian verses and his gestures had been mocked. . . . On entering he had made an obeisance as taught him sixty years ago by the famous dancing master Marcel, and again he had been mocked. He had danced the minuet with the wonted gravity, and that too had drawn ridicule. He had donned his white cocked hat, his gilt lace collar, his black velvet waistcoat, lacing his famous garters about his silk clocked stocking as prescribed —and they had dared to laugh. *'Cospetto!'* he exclaimed. 'Scum, all of you, Jacobins! You refuse obedience to the Count, and the Count does me injury in not chastising you. Sir,' he would turn to the Count, 'I shot the Crown Chamberlain of Poland through the belly. I may not have been born a nobleman, but I have made myself a nobleman.'

The Count would merely laugh at him, more reason for him to complain.

"One day the Count entered his room, carrying a brace of pistols, without saying a word, his face grave, so that he might laugh over his foolish guest. Casanova began to weep, threw himself into the Count's arms and cried: 'How could I kill my benefactor! *Bella cosa!*' He sobbed and whined, accepted the pistols in fear that he might be thought afraid of a duel, returned them with a courageous movement as though offering a lady his hand for the minuet, his fingers raised to his eyes, then broke out into tears again and began to babble about the cabala, magic and . . . macaroni.

"The respectable mothers of the village complained that he annoyed their daughters, filling their heads with silly stuff. He reviled them as democrats. The abbey of Ossegg, half an hour from Dux, he called a second Calvador, for some reason I do not recall, creating discord between the good monks and himself and the Count. Then he would overtax his stomach and claim there had been an attempt to poison him. This, he insisted, was done at the behest of the Jesuits. At Oberleutensdorf the Count owned a cloth-weaving factory, where Casanova obtained goods on credit, subsequently becoming insulted when payment was demanded. . . .

"How could he put up with such continuous 'persecutions'? In the end God bade him leave Dux.

174

Without necessarily believing in God, as he did in his death which he thought imminent at any moment, he still insisted that all he did was done at God's behest. Heaven had commanded him, he said, to ask me for letters of recommendation to Weimar, to the Duke who loved me, to the Duchess of Saxe-Gotha, who does not know me, and to certain Jews in Berlin.

"He left Dux secretely, leaving behind a farewell letter to the Count, gentle, vain, pompous, full of wrath. The Count merely laughed, saying that he would be back. The journey did not agree with him. He was left waiting in antechambers. No one offered him a post as librarian, tutor, chamberlain, or the like. He called the Germans stupid louts, one and all. The estimable Duke of Weimar received him as well as possible, but Casanova at once grew jealous of the Duke's old favorites, Goethe and Wieland, loudly inveighing against them and their works.

"He went on to Berlin, where he ranted against the ignorance of the people, against superstition, against the deceits of the Jews to whom he had been recommended, extracting from them money by means of checks drawn on the Count, which the latter laughingly paid. In the end he returned to Dux, where his benefactor fondly embraced him. . . ."

This character sketch of Casanova in his old age

agrees with the picture that emerges from the adventurer's letters, large numbers of which have survived. There are letters from Count Lamberg to him. They are witty and full of information, but between the lines one reads that the Count, like Prince de Ligne, looked on the old librarian as more or less of an eccentric. The Count's letters, published in German by Gugitz, also deal with music, showing that Casanova's interests in this field persisted into his old age.

On March 26, 1767, the count writes from Augsburg about the "Pythagorean Table." He askes whether not a similar square of musical notes may not be contrived, which, used in various ways, would represent a minuet, a gavotte, a sarabande, a fandango, etc." Here the correspondence between Lamberg and Casanova moves into the sphere of so-called "mechanical music," then a very popular subject. A "method" had been invented at the time for "composing" by means of dice and the famous musician and theoretician Johann Philip Kirnberger had actually written a manual in 1757, purporting to show how compositions could be written mechanically, without either inspiration or musical knowledge (*Der allzeit fertige Polonaisen und Menuettenkomponist*). Such manuals on how to compose waltzes, minuets, and other tunes "with dice" have also been ascribed to Haydn, Mozart, and Philip Emanuel Bach. Little wonder that the notion also ghosted about the imaginative heads of Casanova and Count Lamberg.

In another letter Lamberg asked Casanova for a musical book by A. Goudar, *Remarques sur la Musique et Danse en Lettre de M. G. A. Venise chez Charles Palese*, 1773. Lamberg occasionally turned to frivolity in the field of music, as is to be expected of Casanova's correspondents. On May 25, 1790 he wrote from Brno to the aged librarian of Dux: "Keep a lookout and take pains to inform me on the following subject. Herr Johann Baptist Triklir, first cellist to the Elector at Dresden has presented to the public a method he calls 'indiscordability,' aimed at providing stringed instruments, such as the piano, violin, etc., with permanent tension so that they cannot get out of tune. You will readily believe me that it is not I alone who is interested. I am simply instructing my friend Jacob [Casanova is meant] in a shortcut for getting into the good graces of a pretty woman, who unhappily finds the strings of her theorbo forever slack. You can't deny that such is the plea of a pretty woman. . . ."

Casanova in all likelihood had little cause to complain that his "strings were out of tune" while he was young. But now, no doubt, he could have used the method of the Dresden cellist (who died in that city in 1813). Triklir, together with Schick, Benda, and Hofmann, formed a famous string quartet and wrote two theoretical works. We do not know Casa-

nova's reply to Lamberg's letter. But the old pro-
verb of "No fool like an old fool" could well be applied to the aged Venetian.

On February 25, 1791, Lamberg wrote about the
discovery of a manuscript of ancient Greek music,
supposed to have been found in the Library of the
King of Naples. The historian of music Meibom
(who died in 1711), so Lamberg writes, would have
given its weight in gold, had he known about it.
This affords the Count occasion to complain about
his deafness. "I believe," he writes, "that I should
not so much note my depressing deafness, were
there neither violins nor flutes, and the same applies
to drums and percussion instruments which I prefer to the sweet strains of the harmonica. . . ." Here
Lamberg was quite serious, but a few days later, on
April 9, 1794, the frivolous note crops up again
when he reports to Casanova that Beaumarchais
was working on an opera with a ballet in which "the
seven personified sacraments are to dance their
roles, one after the other. Prepare yourself for seeing the Trinity and the Virgin figure under the
same flag!"

But then he also gives information that is of interest in the history of music. In a letter of March
17, 1790, Lamberg tells Casanova of the famous
Russian hunting music of Count Naryshkin: "Mme.
von Cobenzl included the score in her package to
me. Prince Potemkin purchased it from Naryshkin,

Chief Master of the Hunt, for 2,000 rubles—that is for the forty musicians employed in this orchestra. This music, invented under the direction of Count Naryshkin by the bugler Maresh, a native of Bohemia, is absolutely unique. As I have already said, the group consists of forty persons who blow as many horns or pipes of four different sizes and who play the most difficult symphonies of the great Italian masters by sight. Each of them plays but a single note and it takes forty persons to play a single song. The harmony of these instruments is unbelievable and one must hear them to form an opinion. Marquis Bella and General Kaunitz tell of their marvels. Now that I am perhaps the sole possessor of this curiosity (of which there has been so much ignorant talk in several German journals), I should regard it an obligation, an honor, and a pleasure to send you a copy at the first opportunity if it pleases you to command me."

The copy has not been found among Casanova's papers. Perhaps he never asked for it.

There are other notes that clearly show the vivid interest which the aged librarian retained in matters musical. I have excerpted the more important ones from the Casanova archives at Dux and reproduce them here:

"There is no one in the world incapable of learning music and no one who does not love music. That music is best which pleases the largest number. And no one can be denied the right to judge it. Music has no purpose other than to please the ear. Its effect on the senses, the passions, and the moods of the soul is incidental—a subordinate matter not included in the purpose proper.

"This fascinating art is nature's special boon to man, to convince him that she has not limited herself to granting him only what is necessary and useful. Nature sought to distinguish the sovereign of the Animal Kingdom by means of a bountiful gift he alone can cherish. Thus she has acknowledged the sense of hearing as one without which man would regard himself as far unhappier than if he lacked any of the other senses. But for music he would have been condemned to do no more than to strain his reason.

Music appeals to the whole being of every listener. It evokes no doubt. It is never suspected of lying. It poses no problem to the mind. It is no harbinger of ill tidings. Nor does it flatter, insult, praise or reproach anyone.

Music, finally, is subject to no error of hearing. It is, rather, the cause on account of which the sense of hearing feels itself the peer of the other senses, all of which, for the rest, are endowed with far greated capacities and talents.

"Whence the ease with which music is learned, once one applies oneself to it? How is it that in a single town one readily finds three or four musicians who are outstanding in some field of the art and each of whom enjoys the reputation of being his fellows' superior in his own specialty? Among a hundred painters I have trouble finding even *one* who is really good. I scarcely find one *true* poet in a century. Great architects are rare, great mathematicians even rarer. . . .

(Here the note breaks off, the second page being blank.)

There follow notes that likewise seem to bespeak critical or speculative activities on the part of Casanova:

"*Theorème: Combien de fois l'oreille a-t-il plus d'aptitude à distinguer les sons que l'oeil n'en a à distinguer les objets? L'étude est au génie ce que la taille est au diamant, elle rapetisse en même temps qu'elle épure. . .*

"*La superbe capitale de la cinquième partie du globe. . . . Gluck a beaucoup d'idées simples, quelques pensées et peu d'images. . . .*

"*Piccini, l'Alexandre. . . .*

"*Un de deux son chef d'oeuvre, on ne sait lequel. . . .*

"*Paisiello—Les fils de Graces qu'un satire aurait approché. . . .*

"*Anfossi. Plus déserté sans être plus éloquente, c'est à dire qu'il l'est beaucoup. . . .*

"*Traetta. Ce n'est qu'à force d'esprit que Traetta en impose à l'âme. . . . C'est un mot sans esprit, parce qu'il est sans vérité, puis il n'est pas plaisant, parce qu'on ne doit pas rire d'un ouvrage fait à la nature humaine; mais il le devient peut-être quand on songe à la démangeaison de l'auteur. . . ."*

PLATE 13.   National Theatre (*Altstädter Stände-Theater*) in Prague, Where *Don Giovanni* Was First Performed

PLATE 14.

Casanova's Handwritten Version of the Sextet From the Second
Act of *Don Giovanni* (Fragment)

CHAPTER TWENTY-THREE

THE "MEGAMICRES"

ONE of the characteristic works of Casanova's old age is his novel *Icosameron* (or *Histoire d'Edouard et d'Elisabeth qui passèrent quatre vingt un ans chez les Megamicres*). The first edition is today a book lover's rarity of the first rank. In addition to the copies in the Waldstein Library at Hirschberg, I found two in the Bohemian National Museum in Prague. Casanova labored long and hard over this voluminous utopian novel and it is surely the most important document of his old age. The novel was published in 1787 in Prague by Schönfeld. In 1922 a shorter version was published in German translation by Heinrich Conrad.

"If Casanova's work," this Casanova scholar writes in the preface to his edition, "were nothing but one of the many utopias after the model of Thomas More, one of the countless 'Gulliver's Travels' after Swift, it would be scarcely worth unearthing from limbo. But it is more. It is a work of profound and above all free thought. Even more, it is a most entertaining adventure story—true, one that requires a thoughtful reader but that also fascinates by the deliberate wealth of incident, quite apart from its intellectual content."

Edward and Elizabeth, young brother and sister from England, suffer shipwreck in the Maelstrom and in mysterious fashion reach the hollow interior of the earth, the surface of which is inhabited by the "Megamicres" (Big Littles), whose number runs into the billions. Edward is fourteen, Elizabeth twelve. The urge of nature drives them into each other's arms. Brother and sister become man and wife and become the parents of forty pairs of twins, each consisting of a boy and a girl. In the course of their stay inside the earth, which lasts 324 Megamicre years, or eighty-one ordinary years, the pair and their progeny multiply to more than 600,000 persons who make themselves masters of the Megamicre realm.

Edward and Elizabeth have retained their youthful bloom during their time in Paradise (for that is what Casanova's Megamicre realm is to him). Ultimately they return to the earth's surface and their parents' home in England, in the same mysterious way in which they reached the Megamicre realm. In a company of lords and ladies Edward relates his adventures. His report is taken down in shorthand, and in this fashion an English "novel" is originated which Casanova "translates" into French. Every aspect of the plot stems from the shrewd and imaginative brain of the old Venetian.

The novel is obviously the product of a mind of very broad range. It is crammed with facts from almost every field of contemporary knowledge—even though the name Megamicre was in all likelihood borrowed from Voltaire's novel *Micromegas*.

What Conrad says about the book is quite true. It contains "not a trace of the frivolous adventurer, seducer, gambler, and swindler of the memoirs." Yet sex does play a considerable part, though in a way entirely different from the memoirs. It will be up to the psychologist and psychoanalyst to delve into this work of Casanova's old age for the sexual problems of the aging libertine. His sexuality, expressed in his memoirs in so many turbulent adventures, is here lifted to an entirely different level. The novel hinges on the theme of incest, the hero marrying his own sister and all his descendants doing likewise. In this land of the imagination food continues to be taken in the manner customary in mankind only at the tenderest age. It seems almost as though Casanova had sought to give an ethical or religious basis to his primal sexual instincts. Incest is natural, hence God-given. Among the Megamicres every sexual aspect is reduced to esthetic and natural standards.

In keeping with this spirit, music and the dance play an important part in the life of this fictional people. Sound and melody predominate in the speech of the Megamicres, which consists solely of chanted vowels. Casanova's two protagonists are enraptured by this musical tongue. When Edward has learned the Megamicre language tolerably well, he is asked whether in his opinion the chanted words contribute to the beauty of Megamicre singing, or vice versa. He replies: "When music is beautiful, one pays no heed to the words; but the finest words cannot keep music from being hissed, if it is poor music.

"It is noteworthy that the music of that world altogether lacks words. Music with words is always poor, for it no longer leaves the proper impression on the soul, is no longer able to express the composer's thought. The great Megamicre composers, who are also the real poets, laughed loudly when I told them that our own singers sing songs to which a composer contrived the tones as an accompaniment."

The sound language of the Megamicres is described as follows: Each of the six vowels in use— a, e, i, ü, u, o,—may be written in the seven colors of the rainbow. In other words, there are seven different-hued vowel or tone series, or forty-two different word meanings, word value and tone being closely associated. According to Casanova's calculation, the use of sounded vowels in syllable combinations together with musical intervals permits the formation of 29,470 words. At gatherings and parties among the Megamicres the required keynote that forms the basis of conversation is established by the host.

Casanova also has Edward wax rhapsodic about instrumental music among the Megamicres—music unaccompanied by sounded vowels: "It may certainly be said that the art of music has there reached its highest perfection, for all Megamicres are musicians from birth. The tongue of the Megamicres appeals to the ear, as does ours. But their inmost soul manifests itself in music only when the music reaches kindred souls. In the Megamicres the channel by which the divine harmony of music (vocal or instrumental polyphony) reaches the soul is not merely the sense of hearing but the entire skin that covers their bodies. This is true to such a degree that Megamicres in robes of state or honor often cast them off in order to be able to enjoy the perfect beauty of music without limitation, to open every path for it to the enchanted soul. For there are many things that music alone can say to their souls, and we can form but an abstract concept of the sensual effect of their music."

The conjecture that Casanova occasionally dealt

187

with musical theory gains support also from the manner in which he builds up the Megamicre alphabet. "Their alphabet is a scale of many notes, but distributed as was the fourth with the Greeks and Romans. It starts with a C, then leaps to the seventh, the third, the sixth, the second and the fifth. This order signifies that it is really a matter of singing language rather than music." Undoubtedly Casanova here had the Greek modes in mind, and it would appear that in general ancient music was his ideal. Another hint in this direction is the choice of instruments employed by the Megamicres, "One of which corresponded to a lute, the other to a flute." There is also the matter of Megamicre monophony. "Euphony . . . they call a highly melodious song sung by a single voice without musical accompaniment."

While in the matter of their tone language the Megamicres use a chromatic script, Casanova has the people of his fictional realm employ a system of musical notation borrowed from that of Europe. It will be recalled how he deprecated the French style of beating out the music. In discussing the art of conducting in his novel, he speaks of the "Royal Grand Tonemaster" who "conducted a magnificent tone poem performed by a splendid orchestra. During the music he guided the orchestra solely by means of signs."

On one occasion brother and sister are summoned in audience before the ruler of the fictional underworld. Edward concludes his address by singing a duet with Elizabeth: "We sang a fine duet by Maestro Harris, and the tune greatly pleased the royal couple. We were at once shown the courtesy of a response in the form of vocal music. What music that was! Good God!"

The annals of English music mention a number of composers by the name of Harris. Possibly Casanova had in mind Joseph Harris, organist of St. Martin's Church in Birmingham who died in 1814 at Liverpool.

CHAPTER TWENTY-FOUR

CASANOVA AND THE DANCE

CASANOVA'S main characteristics were his unquenchable erotic temperament and his inexhaustible zest for life. It is only natural that he should have surrendered to the dance whenever he had the opportunity. To our adventurer the dance was always a manifestation of erotic sentiment. What he tells us about dancing and the dancers of his time is of the greatest historical interest to students of the subject.

The first opportunity to distinguish himself as a dancer came to him in the year 1744 on his journey to the Near East when he made the acquaintance of the strange and fantastic adventurer Count Bonneval, known throughout Europe as Achmet Pasha. Achmet Pasha was extravagant in his dress as he was in his amusements. When Casanova visited him he treated the Venetian to a charming performance. Neapolitan slaves of both sexes executed a pantomime, dancing the *calabraise* (a South Italian dance, presumably the *tarantella*). Talk then veered to the Venetian dance, the *furlana*. A Venetian himself, and a fine dancer to boot, Casanova was eager to demonstrate it. But there was no partner, nor a musician who knew the tune. Casanova thereupon seized a fiddle and played the *furlana,* while a search was conducted for a partner and a fiddler. Soon both were found. "The nymph," he reports, "chose her position, I followed suit, and we danced six *furlanas* in succession. I grew very warm and breathless, for there is no more fiery national dance. In the rondo my partner virtually seemed to fly. I was beside myself with amazement, for I could not recall ever having seen the dance so perfectly executed, even in Venice. After a few minutes' rest I approached her in some confusion over my fatigue and said: '*Ancora sei, a poi basta se non volete vidermi a morire.*'"

The *furlana* of which Casanova here speaks was the Venetian national dance, musical and choreographic symbol of Venice in the eighteenth century. It was a wooing dance in six-eighths time, executed by one or two couples with much fire and verve. Man and woman approach and separate while executing the most diverse figures, touching hands to feet, striking out with the arms, and circling about each other. The dance is danced to this day in Friuli, whence it takes its name.

But the classic age of the *furlana* was the eighteenth century. Rousseau mentions it in his *Dictionnaire de Musique,* as does Tuerk in his *Klavier-*

schule. Monsigny included one in his *Aline,* and Grétry mentions it in his memoirs. The most famous *furlana,* however, was the one in Campra's *Fêtes Venetiennes,* an opera on which Casanova expresses himself at unusual length in his memoirs. There is an opening ballet sequence in the opera, entitled *Le Bal,* which illustrates a Venetian ball, and the dancers here execute a *furlana.* In 1742 William Corbett published a series of suites for string orchestra. One of them, entitled *Alla Veneziana,* ends in a *furlana.* At the court of Vienna the *furlana* was danced as early as the seventeenth century, as is shown by a manuscript I found in the National Library there, from the hand of the composer Johann Joseph Hoffer. The characteristic element in this *furlana* is the stereotyped repetition of a single theme at the end of both parts. The melody strongly reminds of another *furlana* which I found in an English square-dance booklet. Thus in the eighteenth century square dances in England were danced to the tune of the *furlana.*

It is a surprising fact that these ancient *furlana* tunes have been preserved down to the present day. They are found in the repertory of Scottish military bands, whence Max Bruch borrowed one for his *Schön Ellen.* The English, who use a lively six-eighths rhythm for their jigs, found the old *furlanas* much to their liking.

It should be mentioned that Johann Sebastian

Bach used the *furlana* in his C-Major Suite and that Wanda Landowska, inspired harpsichordist and connoisseur of ancient music, believes that one of Domenico Scarlatti's sonatas (the one in C-major, L.R. 104) is nothing but a *furlana*. We also find the *furlana* in Mouret's ballet, *Les Amours des Dieux*.

It was surely not the original *furlana* tune that Casanova knew. He remembered a tune something like that used by Campra in his *Fêtes Venetiennes*.

Furlanas also occur in a symphony by the mulatto composer Saint George, where they are repeated no less than twenty times. Yet it is said that at the end of the piece, despite the many repetitions, the listener was left with a sense of regret at no longer hearing the tune. (*"Et à la fin du Morceau on est faché de ne plus l'entendre."*) Perhaps this helps to explain why Casanova was so fascinated by the *furlana* and never grew tired of it.

In his *Handbook of the Dance* the French ballet master Blasis describes the *furlana* as follows: "The dance is the embodiment of love and joy. Animated by the accompaniment of mandoline, tambourines, and castanets, the woman dancer, by her liveliness and pace, seeks to kindle her partner's love. The dancers approach, separate, and in their every gesture express flirtation, love, fickleness."

Mention must still be made of one of the most interesting eighteenth-century books on the dance,

Gregorio Lambranzi's *New and Curious Theatrical School of the Dance* (Nuremberg, 1716). It is an illustrated description of various grotesque dances, showing how they were then executed in the theaters and amusement places of Italy and Germany. Some of these masked dances remind of their later modification, the *cotillon*. Among the various descriptions that of a Venetian mariners' dance is noteworthy. Lambranzi says: "A Venetian seaman or gondolier appears (on a square before one of the magnificent palaces) and dances a *furlana* in the Venetian style. This is a very special *furlana* with a curious, traditional step, and it lasts long enough for the music to be repeated two or three times."

It is interesting that the tune of the *furlana* is also called *polesana*. It is possible that Pola may have been its original source.

The resemblance of this melody to the phrases reproduced by Grétry is obvious. It would appear that this tune, or one like it, was the standard *furlana* of the time.

Casanova frequently reverted to the subject of the *furlana*. During the carnival season of 1754, when he was having his love affair with the Venetian nun, he attended a masked ball in the guise of Pierrot. The ball took place in a convent—one is surprised to learn that nuns used to hold masquerades in their convents. There were many guests, wearing every possible mask from the *commedia dell'arte—Pulcinelli, Pantaloni, Arlecchini, Scaramuccie.* Casanova first danced a minuet with an *Arlecchina,* and then twelve *furlanas,* with the greatest vivacity. . . . Quite out of breath, he allowed himself to recline and pretended to be asleep. The dancing had exhausted him. "There was a quadrille that lasted an hour. Scarcely was it over when an *Arlecchino* came and, banking on the license permitted his costume, began to belabor my back with a wooden sword, his traditional weapon. Since as a Pierrot I was unarmed, I seized him by his belt and carried him about the hall at a run, while he continued to belabor me with his wooden sword. Then the charming *Arlecchina* with whom I had danced came to his aid, likewise treating me to blows. I let go of him, wrested the wooden sword from his hands, merrily hoisted his *Arlecchina* to my shoulders and drove him ahead of me with redoubled blows—to the loud guffaws of the spectators. . . ." Just a little sidelight from an eighteenth-century ball at Venice!

In England the *furlana* became part of the square dance, but in the City on the Lagoon it continued to be danced independently as a folk dance. But let us proceed with Casanova's choreographic biography. Four years after the ball in the convent he attended a ball at Amsterdam, where most of the dances were square dances. We need not tarry over them, since their nature and history are well known.

Of greater interest is the carnival celebration of 1759 at Bonn, given by the Elector of Cologne, which moved Casanova to some very strange reflections.

It was marked by one of the famous "peasant weddings," and this is what Casanova has to say: "We were all disguised as peasants, the costumes coming from a special wardrobe of the Prince. Only *quadrilles* and *allemandes* were danced. Of the ladies present but four or five belonged to high society. All the others, more or less pretty, were in the private party of the Prince. Two of these ladies knew how to dance the *furlana* [it can scarcely be doubted that they were members of the Elector's ballet, recruited in the main from among Italian dancers] and the Elector took endless pleasure in watching us dance." On this occasion Casanova again assures us of his great predilection for this Venetian dance, of which he danced twelve rounds. When the thirteenth came up, he was simply unable to go on. But his spirits were revived when another dance was begun "during which, at a certain passage, one seizes a dancer and kisses her. I let myself go and kissed my fair partner ardently whenever I succeeded in encountering her."

The kissing dance was nothing unusual in Germany. It may have appeared strange to an Italian, though it was not entirely unknown in Italy. In France, Germany, and England kissing during dancing goes back to time immemorial. The *gavotte,* for example, was such a kissing dance and even in the square dances—especially the *allemande*—there was often much license. But there were regular kissing *quadrilles,* like that mentioned by Böhme in his *History of the Dance in Germany:* "The kissing *quadrille* has the curious and quite respectable feature that a kiss is exchanged after the musical introduction. After the conventional figures two opposite couples (joining hands crosswise) advance toward each other. The dancer whirls his partner, hands held over the head, and then there is a pause in the music, during which the kiss is exchanged." From the observation of several writers we may conclude that the kissing dance was a special form of the *allemande, alsacienne, strassbourgoise,* etc., which were then in part danced as figures of the square dance, in part independently.

But before we discuss the *allemande,* the "German Dance," let us revert to the Bonn "peasant wedding," so highly praised by Casanova. The occasion mentioned by the adventurer was a celebration that falls within a certain type of German baroque festival, called "The Inn" (*Wirtschaft*). There are records of such revelries at German courts as far back as the sixteenth century. They were rather different from the French and Italian masked balls, in which the individual was free to choose his own mask. Here masks and partners

197

were determined by the master of ceremonies at the court, who sometimes had lots drawn. It was part of the baroque tradition to submit to higher authority, and this type of festival fitted in well with the baroque spirit.

Each of these festivals had a definite plan, within which the masks were definitely fixed. In "The Inn" the princely couple presided at the head of the table as the innkeeper and his wife, while the guests were served at separate tables by "grooms and maids"—who were, of course, aristocrats and members of the court. The case was similar with the "peasant wedding," in which typical characters of the German village made their appearance—the "scissors grinder," the "village Jew," the "barber." Naturally spirits ran high.

There were other varieties with a make-believe courtly or bucolic background. To the French these German court festivals were something novel at the end of the seventeenth century, and the French writer Menestrier (*Des ballets anciens et modernes selon les règles du théâtre*, Paris, 1682) describes them as follows: "*On fait en Allemagne de ces Festins d'appareil, particulièrement le Carnaval, où les Princes, les Seigneurs et les Dames se déguisent en Hôteliers et Hôtelières, en Valets et Servantes d'hôtelleries ce qu'on nomme Virtschafft.*' Menestrier had witnessed such an event at Munich and speaks of it as "*d'une manière la plus agréable et la plus spirituelle du monde."* The spectacle of the "peasant wedding" at Bonn must have been strange to Casanova, for he remarks ingenuously that "it would have been absurd to choose another costume, since the Elector himself had decided to don it."

Apart from the Italian *furlana,* the danses at these "peasant weddings" were *contredanses* and *allemandes.* It is characteristic, at any rate, that the minuet had already become the dance of the aristocracy, while the common people enjoyed the square dances and "German dances." As Casanova tells the story, the aristocracy of Bonn did not participate in the celebration he witnessed. Similarly, in Mozart's *Don Giovanni* the minuet, then already in fashion, is danced by Don Ottavio and Donna Elvira, while the *allemande,* then new, fresh and still somewhat vulgar, is danced by Leporello and Masetto, representatives of the lower class.

When Prince Bernard of Saxe-Weimar visited the United States in 1825, he spent some time in New Orleans. There was much dancing there. At the balls of "fine society" there were only old-fashioned French *quadrilles.* But the gentlemen never tarried long. They hastened to the balls of the quadroons (mulattos), where cotillons and waltzes were danced—the new, fresh dances. As for the "peasant weddings" with their air of condescension, what else could have been danced there but the *allemande?* For reasons rooted in the mentality of the times, the "German dance" had attained special popularity, for it accorded with the spirit of revolution that was in the air, with the democratic persuasions of the masses. The simultaneous whirling of all the couples was something novel and fascinating. Then too, the music of this dance was fresh, and its movements were natural and appealed to the common people. The "German Dance" actually came from Austria and many of the *Arie Viennesi* of seventeenth-century Austrian dance composers are disguised waltzes. (I myself published specimens of these oldest of the Vienna Waltzes in the *Denkmäler der Tonkunst in Oesterreich.*)

As for Casanova, he danced not only the lively and sometimes lascivious *allemande* but often enough the minuet—especially when he sought to make a good impression as a gentleman. As late as 1763 he danced the minuet in London, though during a wild orgy he had an English woman demonstrate the hornpipe for him, to the music of blind musicians. An approximate idea of the indecency of this dance at the time may be formed—the music was originally played on the bagpipe. True, the hornpipe entered formal music and was used by composers like Purcell, Muffat, Handel, and others. But it was danced with the abdomen to furious movements of the legs.

When Casanova tried his luck in Spain in 1768, he was enthralled by the Spanish national dance, the *fandango*. New police regulations at Madrid had just made public balls the great fashion, and every dancer had to bring his own partner. Casanova had little trouble in finding one for himself. The dance itself he describes in glowing colors, as was his fashion: "Toward midnight I witnessed an altogether entrancing spectacle. To the strains of the music and the clapping of hands the couples lined up for the maddest dance that can be imagined. This was the famous *fandango*, which I thought I already knew, but of which I had in reality no idea. I had heretofore seen it danced but on the stage in Italy and France, and the dancers had evidently taken great care to avoid those movements that make the *fandango* the most enticing and voluptuous dance in the world. It cannot be described. Each couple—man and woman—makes but three steps, clicking the castanets in time with the music. But they assume a thousand positions and make a thousand movements of incomparable sensuality. There are the first sighs of desires and the ultimate ecstasy of fulfillment. . . . the masked gentleman who had taken me to my box told me: 'To get a real idea of the *fandango* you must see it danced by the *gitanas* (gypsies), with men who dance in their own style.'"

Whoever has witnessed dancing in Spain will be well able to bear out Casanova's testimony on its fervor. Casanova was so enamored of the *fandango*

201

that within three days he had learned it so well from an opera dancer that "in the judgment of Spaniards there was no one who could flatter himself to outdo me. . . ." A few days later he exhibited his skill at another ball and there was general surprise to see a foreigner dance so well in the Spanish style. Spaniards have always invested their dancing with more feeling than any other nation. To them social dancing always remains to a certain degree a spectacle, and here too the semioriental origins of the Spanish people are revealed. Hence the important part assigned to gesture and espcially facial expression by Spanish dance theorists such as Don Preciso in his *Elementos de la Ciencia Contredanzaria.*

There are a number of treatises on the theory and origin of the *fandango.* Some authorities trace it to the African *chica.* Others insist it was introduced in Spain only in the seventeenth century from the *Reinos de las Indias*—i.e. from America to Europe, like the *sarabande* and the *folia,* an entirely plausible theory! At any rate, it is characteristic that Casanova's two favorite dances were of an exotic-erotic character—the savage *furlana* and *fandango.*

CHAPTER TWENTY-FIVE

CASANOVA AND DA PONTE

THERE is one man who is particularly noteworthy among Casanova's many friends. One of the most important opera librettists of the eighteenth century, he was the man from whose hands Mozart received the libretto for *Don Giovanni*, that "opera of operas." But more than that, the lives of the two friends were very similar in many respects and interlinked in curious fashion.

Both of them, Casanova and Da Ponte, were members of that group of adventurous Italians represented in the eighteenth century at every court of Europe, in the aristocratic circles of London, Vienna, Paris and Prague. Now they led the lives of great gentlemen, driving in a coach-and-four, giving lavish parties and moving in the company of the fairest women; now they were penniless, borrowing the price of last night's lodging from some old friend. . . .

There was a strange and somewhat mysterious relationship between the author of *Don Giovanni* and Casanova. It seems almost as though Da Ponte deliberately modeled his own life on that of his compatriot, though he never quite succeeded in attaining the goal of his aspirations, perhaps because he lacked the erotic genius with which Casanova was endowed to such a high degree.

Da Ponte was of Jewish descent. His mother was Chella (Rachel) Pincherle, his father Geremia Conegliano Corduangerber. The entire family was baptized on August 29, 1763 by Bishop Lorenzo da Ponte, whose name they assumed. The poet himself was born Emanuele Conegliano on March 10, 1749, in Ceneda, Vittorio Veneto. Like Casanova, little Lorenzo had been destined for the cloth. And like Casanova, he suffered moral shipwreck for the first time in the iridescent immorality of the great Mediterranean metropolis, Venice. He became enmeshed in the charms of beautiful women and learned to drain the pleasures of life to the dregs. Again like Casanova, he found rich soil for his natural bent toward amorous adventure. It was in Venice that Casanova actually became the prototype of Don Giovanni, and it was there too that Da Ponte grew familiar with the Don Giovanni atmosphere he later depicted in such masterly fashion in his libretto to Mozart's great opera.

Love, man's primal motive, was ever-present in

the remote side canals, in the boudoirs of the Venetian palaces, in the rooms of the *Ridotto*, Venice's notorious gambling hell, in the nooks and crannies and narrow streets—even in the sacred precincts of the nunneries. The ecstasy of the Venetian carnival, the lush festivities of the magic city, already doomed, bewitched them both—Casanova and Da Ponte.

Venice soon grew too hot for Da Ponte, as it had for Casanova. The latter, in his open and unrestrained manner, had hurled himself with untroubled passion and audacity into a whirl of adventures with women, gamblers, and notabilities, as whose peer he regarded himself. But Da Ponte, burdened with the mentality of an ancient race, proceeded with greater caution and restraint. He too was shadowed by his oath of chastity and celibacy, though this did not keep him from amours, seductions, and adulteries. But there is a vast difference between the memoirs of Casanova and those of Da Ponte. Casanova was generous, profligate, an exhibitionist inclined to exaggeration and invention. Da Ponte held back a great deal—his memoirs are an apologia for his life.

The manner in which the two men present their departure from Venice is typical. Casanova's escape from the Leads of the Palace of the Doges became famous throughout the world. He boasts of this escapade as he does of many other questionable adventures. He does not shrink from laying bare his adventure with the nun and the later Cardinal Bernis, the French Ambassador—the very incident that earned him his arrest by the Venetian tribunal. And what about Da Ponte? His adventures in Venice were not quite so sensational, yet at bottom the life he led here did not greatly differ from that of Casanova. He too was indicted and had to make his escape. But he is silent on the true reasons, insisting that the charge against him was that he had eaten meat on Friday. Actually a rival of his had brought suit for adultery and concubinage, and he was sentenced to seven years in the dungeon. Da Ponte mentions this no more than many other things. . . . And let us not forget, Da Ponte wrote his memoirs in New York, against a Puritan background that made him want to forget the worst defections of his life. . . .

Both Casanova and Da Ponte were highly talented in a literary sense. But Casanova made little use of his talents in his youth—not until his old age did his poetic and philosophic vein flow freely. Da Ponte was a poet from youth. He wrote poems and improvised, occasionally even performing in the public squares, the coffee houses, and the taverns. When he went to Treviso and later to Görz, his classical education and poetic talent stood him in good stead. But his gift for the theater did not come to his own attention until relatively late.

At Görz Da Ponte had a rival, a printer and author, who, according to Da Ponte, forged a letter from the Dresden court librettist, Cattarino Mazzolà, enticing him to Dresden on the pretext that there was a post for him there. This became the occasion for Da Ponte to interest himself more intensively in writing for the theater. At Dresden he became assistant to Mazzolà whom he helped, among other things, in his work on the Masonic opera *Osiris* composed by Naumann. It was perhaps for this reason that he later suggested the writing of a Masonic opera to Mozart—*The Magic Flute*.

But in Dresden too intrigues prevented an extended sojourn. Da Ponte went to Vienna, where he found the century's greatest librettist, Metastasio, on his deathbed, so to speak. Da Ponte thought that he could fill Metastasio's shoes! He got as far as Emperor Joseph II in person, offering his services as official theater poet. The Emperor asked him how many plays he had already written. "Your Majesty," came the brazen but sincere reply, "none!" "Fine, fine," Joseph retorted, "we shall have a virginal Muse"—and the onetime *abbé* was hired as Imperial Poet of the Theater.

This was the beginning of Da Ponte's great career as a librettist. His friend was the composer and Court Orchestra Conductor Antonio Salieri, the man who had opened the Emperor's door to him. Salieri carried great influence in Vienna. He owed this influence originally to the protection of Gluck. His intrigues against Mozart were much discussed and later on there was even a baseless rumor in circulation that he had poisoned the great master, from jealousy.

It was for Salieri that Da Ponte wrote his first libretto, but before he set to work, he studied the literature in the field. He visited the librettist Varesi who did not permit him to take home a single one of his valuable books, but did let him study them in Varesi's own home. Da Ponte's opinion of the art of the libretto in his time was devastating. But when he set to work to write a piece of his own, he began to realize the enormous difficulties in the way of his undertaking. In the end it was not *his* play, *Il Ricco d'un Giorno,* that was performed, but that of the Italian poet Giovanni Battista Casti, *Il Ré Theodoro,* with music by Paisiello.

But this had the advantage that he could now study the art of the libretto even more intensively. The premiere of his *Il Ricco d'un Giorno,* with music by Salieri, was a failure, it is true. It earned him scorn mockery on the part of his adversaries who had soon appeared on the scene in Vienna. But it would seem that Da Ponte continued to enjoy the Emperor's favor, and soon there was a Casti

party and a Da Ponte party. The emperor favored
Da Ponte, but the Director of Theaters, Count Orsini-Rosenberg, favored Casti. Then good fortune
seemed about to smile on the onetime *abbé*, but a
love affair became the cause for a year's illness that
cost him all his teeth; a rival, who practiced dentis-
try, "cured" him with a poison. . . . He grew reconciled to his fate only with the success of his opera,
Il Burbero di buon cuore (January 4, 1786), to
which the Spaniard Vincenzo Martin had written
the music. "We have conquered," the Emperor
whispered in his ear, meeting him at the theater
exit.

Prominent among the wealthy art patrons of
Vienna was Baron von Wetzlar, who came from a
Jewish family. In his salon Da Ponte met Mozart
who had long been looking for a good librettist.
The meeting must have taken place as early as 1783,
as evidenced from a letter of Mozart's, dated May 7,
1783 and addressed to his father. Mozart described
it as follows: "There is a certain *Abbé* Da Ponte
here, a poet. He is furiously busy at the theater, has
been obliged to write an entirely new book for Salieri [*Il Ricco d'un Giorno*, December 14, 1783],
which will not be done for at least two months. He
has promised then to write a new one for me. Who
knows whether he can and will keep his word? You
probably know, these fine Italians are always very
nice to your face. Alas, we know them! If he has an

understanding with Salieri, I shall never get anything in all my born days."

Well, in this instance the Italian kept his promise. It would seem that the Jewish baron had a
hand in the agreement between Mozart and Da
Ponte, from which *The Marriage of Figaro* was to
spring. But first Da Ponte had to write the opera
Il finto Cieco (February 20, 1786) for Giuseppe
Gazzaniga, a translation of *L'aveugle clairvoyant* by
LeGrand after de Brosse. Da Ponte says that it was
a shoddy piece of music and verse. It was a kind of
pasticcio—a medley from various operas by Gazzaniga.

But this failure had no effect on Da Ponte's activities. A talk with Mozart called his attention to
Beaumarchais' comedy which Mozart seemed to like
very much. Da Ponte declared himself willing to
recast it as an opera. Baron von Wetzlar contributed
a fee and offered to have the opera produced in
London or France, should it be suppressed in
Vienna. For *Figaro* had already been rejected by
the Emperor as "not being quite decent enough for
a respectable audience." I do not know whether it
has been previously noted that Wetzlar, the Jew
and a representative of the "new aristocracy," here
unquestionably sought to get in a dig against the
high aristocracy, which comes off rather poorly in
Figaro.

Again it was Emperor Joseph who encouraged

Da Ponte in his undertaking. The ensuing plots that were hatched in order to foil production of the opera are well known and may be read in any Mozart biography.

Da Ponte also wrote the operas *Il Demargogone overo il Filosofo confuso* for the composer Vincenzo Righini (July 12, 1786), *Gl'Equivoci* for Storace and *Il Bertoldo* (June 22, 1787) for Francesco Piticchio. His greatest success up to then had been the opera *Una Cosa rara,* with music by the Spaniard Martin y Soler, which was produced on November 17, 1786, to frenzied applause. It was long believed that in this opera the first waltz was danced on the stage.

Da Ponte's mortal enemy Casti had been banished from Vienna, and Count Rosenberg, the Director of Theaters, had changed his mind and was treating Lorenzo more graciously than before. Thus the poet's spirits rose, and since Mozart, Salieri, and Martini were all urgently demanding librettos, he resolved to write three at the same time. For Salieri he wrote an adaptation of Beaumarchais' *Tarare,* an opera produced on January 8, 1788, under the title of *Assur, Ré d'Ormus.* For Martini he wrote *L'Arbore di Diana,* a work that came out on October 1, 1787. Da Ponte himself seems to have been quite in love with this opera, describing it as his best work. The theme was very "voluptuous"—and this was because Da Ponte, as he expressly says, wanted to please the court. Diana's garden, in which chastity reigns, is transformed by Amor into a garden of love. As for Diana's tree, its apples shine and its branches give forth heavenly music whenever the nymphs walk under it in seemly chastity. But in the end Diana herself succumbs to the blandishments of love and has the tree felled. . . .

The aristocrats of Prague, following the great success which *Figaro* scored in the Bohemian capital, had commissioned Mozart to write another opera. Da Ponte and Mozart chose the theme of Don Giovanni. Thus Da Ponte was writing two texts surcharged with eroticism at the same time. A fair girl of sixteen was then waiting on the poet and what took place between them is hinted at by Lorenzo in his memoirs merely by means of asterisks. . . . Indeed, he had to beg her to lessen the frequency of her visits, since she was too affectionate and a past mistress in the art of love. . . . There was a flask of Tokay wine that stood on the desk of the poet at all times for refreshment purposes. One cannot suppress the thought that these circumstances may not have been quite unimportant in the writing of the libretto. At any rate, the very text of *Don Giovanni* was written in a highly erotic atmosphere.

Reading Da Ponte's memoirs, one encounters Italian names time and again. It was the Italians who dominated music and the theater, who crowded the coffee houses and taverns of Vienna, who held

a prominent place in the book trade. In the field of
science too they bulked large. Time and again we
run into the literary, adventurous type of Italian.
These Italians were internationally minded, frequented the same circles, the same cafés, the same
bookshops, and it was quite natural that Casanova
and Da Ponte should know each other—know each
other well.

Da Ponte devotes much space to Casanova in his
memoirs. The man and his life evidently had long
fascinated him. He reports that he first met Casanova in Venice in the year 1777, in the house of the
Venetian aristocrats Memmo and Zaguri. One of
the two Memmo brothers, Bernardo, was Lorenzo's
patron, while the other, Andrea, was a friend of
Casanova's of long standing. The two men, Casanova and Da Ponte, fell out on account of some controversy and did not meet again until the year 1785
in Vienna. Da Ponte tells that one day in Vienna
he had a dream about meeting Casanova and Salieri
on the *Graben*. When Salieri came to call for his
librettist for their wonted walk and the two had
reached the *Graben,* they met an old man who approached them in great agitation, exclaiming: "Da
Ponte, Da Ponte, what a pleasure to see you again!"

"He remained in Vienna for several years," Lorenzo continues in his memoirs, "but neither I nor
anyone else knew what he was doing or how he was
making his living. I often talked with him, and he

always found my house and purse open. Although I found myself unable to approve of his principles and his mode of living, I nevertheless paid close heed to his counsel and precepts. I realize now that they were exceedingly valuable—truly golden rules. Unfortunately I followed them too little. I could have derived the greatest profit from them, had I applied them more often. . . ."

The importance Da Ponte attributes to Casanova and his counsel is curious. Da Ponte was deeply impressed by Casanova and seems to have emulated him, despite his objections to his friend's "principles." As a matter of fact, Da Ponte gives much more space in his memoirs to Casanova than to many far more important contemporaries with whom he was in touch. Not even Mozart, of whose friendship Da Ponte was very proud, rates as much space as Casanova.

Da Ponte also mentions the "magnificent fraud" in the life of Casanova. He tells that one day in Vienna—it must have been the year 1785—he was walking in the *Graben* with Casanova when his friend suddenly flew into a state of great agitation. He went straight for a man and shouted at him: "Ah, bandit, so I have finally found you! Casanova seized hold of the man and there was a fight to which Da Ponte put an end by leading Casanova away by the hand. Casanova had recognized the

PLATE 15.
Lorenzo Da Ponte, Mozart's Librettist and Casanova's Friend

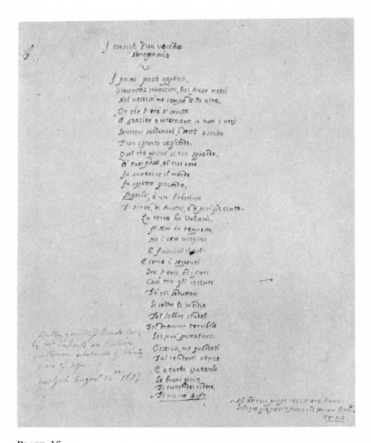

PLATE 16.

Poem Written by Lorenzo Da Ponte as a Nonagenarian, and
Dedicated to Miss Dard, a Young American Lady

man as his old servant Costa who years ago in Paris had cheated him of the fruits of his fraud against the Marquise d'Urfé. Costa, who had meanwhile turned "poet" and was in the service of an Austrian aristocrat in this capacity, vanished into a coffee house and sent Casanova the following poem:

Casanova, non far strepito,
Tu rubesti, ed anch'io furboi,
Tu maestro, ed io discepolo
L'arte tua bene imparai.
Desti pan, ti io focaccia,
Sera meglio che tu taccia.

(Casanova, grow not heated,
You have stolen, I have cheated.
You the master, I the student,
In your art I too am prudent.
You gave me bread, I gave you cake—
Hold your tongue, for Heaven's sake!)

"These verses," Da Ponte relates, "took excellent effect. After a brief silence, Casanova began to laugh and whispered into my ear: '*Il birbante ha ragione*' (the scoundrel is right). He entered the café and waved to Costa to come out. They walked together down the *Graben* as though nothing had happened and finally parted after shaking hands several times. Casanova rejoined me and showed me his cameo ring which by a strange coincidence represented Mercury, patron saint of the thieves.

This trinket was the last remnant of Costa's rich haul. It seemed to fit the character of the two reconciled friends excellently...."

Reading the letters of the aged Casanova, as collected by Molmenti, Rava, and Gugitz, one sees that Casanova, too seems to have had a strange interest in Da Ponte. When the rumor spread that the Emperor, because of the war against the Turks, was about to dissolve the Italian Opera, Casanova wrote to Count Collalto on March 2, 1789: "I should like to know whether *Abbé* Da Ponte will stay. He no longer writes me—he is irked because I failed to praise his work. A flatterer is no friend." On January 4, 1790, he wrote to the same addressee: "I had to laugh about Ferraresi and the poet's wonted frankness. I think he must have been very disappointed not to show himself on the stage." What the poet's "frankness" referred to in this instance is not clear. The singer Ferraresi at the time was Lorenzo's mistress, singing the lead in *Cosi fan tutte*. It was she on whose account Da Ponte fell into disfavor with Emperor Leopold II and had to leave Vienna. Somewhat later, on April 10, 1790, Casanova again wrote the Count that he was sorry to see Da Ponte lose his post, "though he has forgotten me."

But back to Da Ponte as a librettist. On October 29, 1787, Mozart's new opera with Da Ponte's text was first performed in Prague. *Don Giovanni* was a roaring success. The librettist had hastened to Prague for the rehearsals and a note in the official *Prager Oberpostamtszeitung* of October 8 reports: "The Imperial and Royal Poet, *Abbé* Laurenz Da Ponte, a native Venetian, has arrived from Vienna to spend several days here."

He did spend several days, taking part in the rehearsals at the National Theatre, later the *Stände-Theater*. But, as he himself tells us, "I was obliged to return to Vienna before the curtain rose on the opera." His sojourn in the Bohemian capital came to an end because of an urgent letter from Salieri, whose opera *Assur* was to be produced by Imperial edict on the occasion of the marriage of Archduke Francis. Mozart was without his Italian stage director. This is the starting point for the mysterious incident that precipitated Casanova directly into the background of the greatest of all operas.

In his book, *Rococo Images* (1871) the poet Alfred Meissner tells that Casanova and Mozart had met at a party given by the Prague singer Josephine Duschek, Mozart's friend, in her villa, *Bertramka*, near Prague. Meissner, who was also a historian, states that his sketches were based on notes of his grandfather, the Prague university professor and writer Gottlieb August Meissner (1753-1807). But before we discuss this meeting, so well described by

Meissner, we should try to ascertain whether Casanova, then Count Waldstein's librarian at Dux, was actually in Prague during the premiere of *Don Giovanni*.

This memorable event took place on October 29, and on November 4 Count Lamberg wrote from Brno to the Bohemian writer J. F. Opitz at Czaslau: "Casanova is in Prague. His letter to me is dated October 25." Thus there can be no doubt that Casanova *was* in the Bohemian capital. He was at the time negotiating with the publisher Schönfeld about his novel *Icosameron*. Unquestionably there were connections between him and Mozart. The subscribers' register for *Icosameron* contains a number of names we encounter also in Mozart's life. Let us mention but one, Count Pachta, for whom Mozart wrote his Prague *German Danses*. I found a few pages in the Casanova archives that show the close social relationship between Casanova and Pachta.

At a supper given by Countess Pachta in 1787 Casanova was asked to show off his poetic skill by reciting some impromptu verses addressed to his hostess. He did not respond, for that night the Countess' praises had already been sung by another poet who was present. But the very next day he did send her a poem of sixty-four lines, beginning as follows: "To Countess Canal-Pachta. If, Gracious Lady, thou wishest to know why last night I de-

clined . . ." And on March 17 she received a birthday poem from Casanova, which ended with these
words, characteristic of the aging adventurer: "By
all the world abandoned, excepting only love."

CHAPTER TWENTY-SIX

A PARTY AT THE BERTRAMKA

BUT now to Meissner's description of the meeting of Mozart, Casanova, and Da Ponte. It tells the story of Mozart's writing of the overture to *Don Giovanni,* which he had delayed to the last minute. Mme. Bondini, the original Zerlina and wife of the Prague theater director Bondini (a letter of Casanova's to his nephew Carlo shows that they were friends), managed to persuade Mozart to write down the overture by means of a ruse. The occasion was one of the well-known "evenings at Villa Duschek." According to Meissner, Da Ponte, and Casanova were present. The whole party was worried about Mozart's unconcern in the matter. "Maestro Amadeo, however, pretended not to hear the hints and apparently listened closely to the conversation between Signor Casanova and *Abbé* Da Ponte on the one hand, and Duschek and the singers, on the other.

"Signor Casanova had been presented to the com-

pany under the title of Librarian to Count Waldstein at Dux and Oberleutensdorf. He was a man
in his sixties, of herculean stature and erect bearing.
It was evident that he looked back on a mysterious
past, and he seemed to know the whole world. Not
very long before, he had published a little book in
Prague in the French language, describing his mi-
raculous escape from the Leads of Venice. Now he
was having a three-volume novel entitled *Icosameron* printed there, in the same language.

"In Casanova and Da Ponte two men confronted
each other who had much in common. Both had
spent their youth in Venice. Both had roamed the
world restlessly. Both showed an unmistakable trait
of vanity. They liked to boast of the honors that had
come to them, to mention the potentates they had
met. When the former would come out with his
Frederic of Prussia or Catherine the Great, the latter was sure to bring up Joseph II. Da Ponte, however, clearly had the advantage. He was able to
boast of a favor that still existed, whereas it was
notable in the case of Casanova that the monarchs
who had taken so much pleasure in him and bestowed distinctions on him had let him go again.
Da Ponte was the official 'Theater Poet' at Vienna
and thus the object of much attention on the part
of the ladies, each of whom was ambitious to leave
Prague for the first stage in the German realm.

" 'Do you know, dear *Abbé*,' the mother of Micelli [the original Donna Elvira], a Neapolitan and a typical old theater mother, turned to Da Ponte, one of her purposes being to annoy Saporiti [the original Donna Anna] who had never succeeded in obtaining an engagement at a court theater—'do you know, dear *Abbé*, that my daughter is destined to be engaged by a great court theater?'

" 'My, my,' Da Ponte remarked, 'Guardasoni won't like that. Which court theater is it, if I may inquire?'

" 'I do not yet know myself. But the matter can scarcely be long in coming. Perhaps you have heard of the famous woman on the *Pohorzoletzplatz* who reads the future from her cards? Three times she has found in her cards that my Marie is destined to become a royal court singer—and the most incredible predictions of this woman come true!'

" 'But my dear lady,' Da Ponte rejoined, 'there's nothing incredible about this one! Why should not Signora Marie fill a post at a court theater in worthy fashion? True, it would be better, had she received the assurance from the court orchestra conductor himself, for cards are made of paper and a valid contract, at any rate, is better. But in anticipation of a contract such a prophecy is at least something.'

"Signor Casanova had listened with a grave face. He at once asked for the address of the fortuneteller and told how often he had witnessed the prophecies of such good old women to come true. He said that

222

in his opinion these fortunetellers were visionary women who are translated into a state of somnambulism by shuffling the cards and lifting them and turning them over.

"To the accompaniment of such talk groups began to form for a tour of the garden.

" 'The *Abbé* seems to be a gentleman of high birth,' Micelli remarked to Casanova. 'He said a while back: "My good uncle, the Bishop." '

" 'Don't be fooled!' Casanova retorted. 'You can see, after all, that he is of Israelitic stock. He was a poor Jewish lad who lost his parents at an early age and was put into a seminary that was under the direction of the Bishop of Cenada. Since then he has grown accustomed to pretending that the Bishop is his uncle.'

" 'You don't say! So he is a baptized Jew! But he has taken vows, hasn't he?'

" 'Nevertheless I should not advise you to be married by him,' Casanova remarked with upraised finger. 'I'm afraid the marriage would be no more valid than if I myself had performed it. . . .' "

" 'Signor Casanova seems to be a dignified old gentleman,' Saporiti said meanwhile to Da Ponte. 'And he must have occupied some high positions at various courts. . . .'

" 'You are very mistaken,' Da Ponte retorted. 'He is an adventurer who has lived all his life by card-playing, elixir-brewing and soothsaying. True, he is

223

a shrewd man, and a smooth customer. Since I saw him last he seems to have risen to the nobility, but I do not doubt that his patent is from his own hand.'

" 'You Italians are always slandering each other!' Duschek [the Prague composer and husband of Josephine Duschek, Mozart's friend] entered the conversation.

" 'There are Italians and Italians,' Da Ponte replied. 'Can I say of Casti that he is a man of honor? Can I say of Salieri that he is to be trusted? Casanova says that he is preoccupied with the cabala. Does that mean that for his sake I must regard the cabala as a serious science? My dear friend, hereabouts one can let oneself go, but among my compatriots one must be on one's guard. I did not always do so, and my carelessness has brought me much harm. The Italians, my dear Duschek, are too clever. That is why they are past masters in the art of deception. I trust none of them and I don't like any of them.'

"And he continued: 'As for Salieri—well, I write for the theater, and I give him my librettos as I do to Mozart, but my heart belongs to Mozart, and I have a feeling that only those operas of mine will come down to posterity that he has set to music. Then too, I give him the texts I like best.'

"I'm going to tell the coachmen to harness the horses,' cried Guardasoni [the theater director]. 'It's four o'clock and the sun will soon set. Let us

drive back and leave Mozart alone. I don't know
how he expects to get done with the overture by
tomorrow.'

" 'So it stands that the show goes on the day after
tomorrow, with the last rehearsal tomorrow?' Micelli asked.'

" 'What does the maestro say?' Guardasoni asked.

" 'That's certainly the way it stands!' Mozart replied. 'Otherwise there will be another delay, on account of All Saints' and All Souls' Days. Da Ponte
and I have already had enough trouble with you.
I'm sick of rehearsals. You all know the trouble I've
had with Bondini [the original Zerlina], for example, trying to teach her that scream for help in
the finale of the first act. It has gone tolerably well
with you, my ladies, but as for Bassi [the original
Don Giovanni], I have often wished he were in the
hell to which he ultimately descends.'

" 'I still say that I don't have a single real aria in
the whole opera,' the singer retorted defiantly.

" 'You're a silly boy, Bassi,' Mozart replied. 'Let
things be as they are. Sing and play your part and
let me take care of the music.'

"Turning to the ladies, he said: 'You have a corner for me in the carriage, don't you?'

" 'Mozart, you don't mean to say that you want
to go to Prague today!' Bondini inquired as though
he had heard the worst.

" 'I certainly do. I promised a few friends to meet

225

them at the *Tempelgässchen* [a favorite retreat of Mozart's.]'

" 'Heavens above! The *Tempelgässchen*! You never get away from there before midnight! Be reasonable, Mozart . . . the overture. . . .'

" 'It's done. . . .'

" 'I know you! Done in your head—but nothing has been put down on paper. Look, Mozart, suppose you *can* get it finished by tomorrow noon, the parts have to be transcribed—the overture must be rehearsed.'

" 'Quite true! But I'll get it finished when I get to it at midnight. My friends are expecting me.'

" 'It's awful!' Bondini cried, grouping all the singers and even the Duscheks about him. 'There never has been such recklessness since the beginning of the world. Friends, friends,' he said in a subdued voice, 'there's no other way out, something must be done.'

" 'But what, what?'

" 'We'll have to lock the bird up.'

" 'Excellent! But how shall we get him to his room?'

" 'Child's play!' Mme. Bondini exclaimed. 'Dear maestro, I have left my gloves on the piano. Would you be kind enough to fetch them for me?'

" 'Gladly!' Mozart replied and disappeared into the house. Within a few minutes he appeared at the window and called out: 'I can't find them!'

226

" 'I'll have to go and look myself!' Mme. Bondini replied, and instantly the whole company trouped up the stairs.

" 'There they are!' the singer cried, apparently rummaging among the music. Then she suddenly opened the piano and pleaded: 'Mozart! Just a few chords from the overture! Just a few chords!'

"Mozart sat down and struck a few loud, resounding chords. He had not the least inkling that a conspiracy was afoot against him. The company retired on tiptoe. The door was opened noiselessly, and one by one they left the room. Mozart did not wake up to what was happening until the door clicked shut. He jumped up. 'What's the matter? What does this mean?'

" 'You're a prisoner and will have to spend the night here in your room instead of in the *Tempelgässchen*.'

" 'But what have I done?'

" 'Harken to the verdict of the court!' exclaimed the merry Saporiti. 'Wolfgang Amadeus Mozart, a poor debtor who has long owed us the overture to his opera, thereby gravely imperiling his own interest and ours, is hereby sentenced to several hours' arrest, during which he will be required to pay off his debt.'

" 'But ladies, surely you will grant me the boon of your company for a while!' Mozart cried, appearing at the window beneath which the whole company had gathered. 'How can I write without light, without food and drink?'

" 'It's no use, you're caught. If you want to get out soon, get to work. You shall have light, and wine, and even a large cake. Nothing shall be found wanting.'

" 'This is a betrayal!' Mozart exclaimed. 'I can't bear solitude. What if I were to take my life from melancholy? What if I were to leap from the window? . . .'

" 'We're not worried about that. You have far too much zest for life, little Amadeo!' cried Micelli.

" 'And you, Duschek, you tolerate this?' Mozart began, turning to his friend who was almost hidden behind the group.

" 'We mean well! Truly, truly!' Duschek said.

" 'There you have it—well-wishers approving everything, even treason,' Mozart cried, now really concerned that they would leave him locked up. His face had turned grave, but he could not suppress a smile when he saw the singers who had now formed a procession. They had each taken one of the long vineyard staves that lay in a corner of the courtyard, and to the end of each was tied one of the objects the prisoner might need for the night. 'Here are two candlesticks! Here are a couple of bottles of Melnik wine! Here is some cake and pastry!' the voices cried, proffering the objects named and holding them up to the window sill. As

228

for Da Ponte, who was in even higher spirits than the rest, he appeared with a rake to which he had tied an essential but unmentionable object. 'Here,' he cried, 'is something you may also need during the night. Receive it, O heavenly maestro!'

" 'Alas, that it is empty!' Mozart replied. 'Otherwise you would fare ill.' Torn between anger and amusement, he stood among the uplifted objects.

" 'And you, Signor Casanova,' he cried, 'you who once suffered in the Leads of Venice, who know the torments of a prisoner, you are ready to see me languish here? You will not abstract the key that jeering witch there is holding up? Aye, you were never in prison!'

" '*Pazienzia, caro maestro!*' the old man replied.

" 'At least let my wife share my prison!' Mozart exclaimed. 'Shall I sing you the Plea of the Demons from Gluck's *Orfeo*? Surely you won't be crueler than they!"

" 'The end hallows the means!' Guardasoni cried. 'Good night, Mozart. Tomorrow morning early we shall all come to inquire whether the overture is done.'

" 'Yes, yes, all of us!' cried the girls. 'Good night, sweet Amadeo, good night! Now get to work!'

"Thus the high-spirited company bantered with immortal genius. For genius walks the earth in mortal form, often humbler than others, and only at certain moment can one behold the crown on its head, shining like flames of fire.

"As for Mozart, he was by no means happy over the prank that had been played him. He was in less of a mind to write down the overture than ever. He paced the room, bit his lips, and finally sat down on the sofa in displeasure. Suddenly the key turned in the lock, the door opened, and the towering figure of Casanova appeared on the threshold.

" 'Maestro,' he said, 'you must forgive the jest a high-spirited company has permitted itself. Your kindness and indulgence made them exuberant, but they really mean well. They think you will sit down and compose, if only you are behind lock and key. They do not realize that your annoyance may well have dispelled all inspiration. Mozart himself must be the best counselor of his fame. He knows best what he must do. Hence I have taken the key from Bassi and now liberate you from your dungeon.'

" 'You seem to me to be the most sensible person in the group.' Mozart replied, offering Casanova his hand. 'I thank you.'

" 'It was the ladies who hatched the plot,' Casanova said. 'Just appear unexpected in their midst and extract a kiss from every one—that will be the best punishment.'

" 'Thank you, Signor Casanova,' Mozart replied. 'You may do so on my behalf. I shall stay here, and tomorrow the world shall have the overture.'

"He kept his word. Guardasoni was kept awake

by feverish unrest and had his horses harnessed as
early as four o'clock in the morning. He drove out
to Duschek's villa and saw light in Mozart's room,
a sign that the composer was still at work. By seven
o'clock the overture was finished. It was immediately handed to several copyists so that the parts
could be transcribed."

CHAPTER TWENTY-SEVEN

CASANOVA'S CONTRIBUTION TO
DON GIOVANNI

IT must remain a matter of conjecture whether Meissner's dialogue is fictional or not. It is certain, at any rate, that Da Ponte was in Prague on neither October 28 or 29, for according to his own testimony he had been called back to Vienna before the premiere. But could not the meeting described by Meissner have occurred earlier?

As has already been mentioned, Casanova had come from Dux to Prague in order to conduct negotiations concerning his *Icosameron*. But he must also have been tempted to meet Da Ponte and witness the premiere of *Don Giovanni,* which bade fair to be the great event of the season.

His librettist having been recalled to Vienna, Mozart was without the aid of an Italian author or literary man to supervise the singers. What could have been more natural than for Da Ponte to ask his friend Casanova to take over his place?

There is no unequivocal evidence that this is actually what happened. There are only two pages in Casanova's hand that tell us of the active interest he took in the opera. I found these pages years ago in Dux, together with the Casanova scholar Bernhard Marr. They show a reworking of the sextet from the opera's second act in Casanova's handwriting.

What is the story behind this Casanova manuscript? The old adventurer must certainly have been deeply impressed by the libretto. We can well imagine that listening to the *Catalogue Aria* or reading Da Ponte's text he saw his own life story rise up before him like a vision of the past. Da Ponte's theme fitted him to a hair! The feminine characters in the opera seemed to have been borrowed from his own life! And Leporello, Don Giovanni's servant—did he not recall Casanova's own servant Costa who had loved and at once deceived him? With fear and trembling the old reprobate may have taken Don Giovanni's end to foreshadow his own.

Small wonder that in his version of the sextet he has Leporello exclaim: "The guilt comes home to the female sex alone, which cast a spell over his soul and heart. O tempting sex!" But immediately afterward Leporello accuses his master. The conclusion of the whole piece is a farce. The gallows, the dungeon, the club, the penalty of keelhauling threaten from the pursuers. And Leporello calls back: *"Sono d'illustre razza!"* (Not bad from the viewpoint of Casanova, who had assumed the aristocratic title of de Seingalt.)

It is another question whether Casanova actually intended to substitute his own text to Mozart's music. It woud have been quite like this literary mountebank and clever versifier. Or was Casanova's text meant for an "improvisation"? We know that there was much improvisation at Prague during the performance of *Don Giovanni*. If we may believe the imaginative deaf author, painter and musician Johann Peter Lyser, Luigi Bassi, the original Don Giovanni, reported that there was always much improvisation under Guardasoni, then theater director; and Mozart himself is supposed to have been much given to improvisation, especially in the dinner scene. Why should not Casanova's version too have been performed?

The significance of the connection between Mozart and Casanova becomes clearer when we approach the meeting between the two men, of which we have but fragmentary evidence, from a higher aspect—symbolically and so to speak metaphysically. Their relationship seems to express the erotic flamboyance of an age that went into eclipse with Mozart's *Don Giovanni* and Casanova's memoirs. We certainly do not mean to lump the lubricity and exhibitionism of Casanova's adventures with the heavenly strains of Mozart. But the ultimate background of both works is the same. In Casanova we meet this state of mind in its materiel, sensual, worldly aspect. With Mozart it crystallized to divine sublimity.

Soren Kierkegaard has evaluated the Don Juan theme, "uniquely musical in the deeper sense," describing it as rare good fortune that it was entrusted to Mozart, of all composers, just as the theme of the Trojan War, the epitome of the epic, was reserved to Homer. Kierkegaard saw in Mozart the master of musical eroticism, demonstrating its various gradations by examples—Cherubin's intoxication with love, Papageno's robust naturalness. We might add the crass sensuality of Monostato and the erotic genius of Don Giovanni. In *Don Giovanni* the "erotic age" receives its apotheosis, in Casanova's memoirs its documentation.

There is a deep symbolic meaning in the fact that Casanova was present at the premiere of the "opera of operas" and presumably even participated in its staging, while at the same time there is a complete lack of any historical or documentary evidence for any relationship between Mozart and Casanova. It is as though the genius of history sought to tell us: "Let mankind forget that the two spoke the same tongue."

Here is he text of Casanova's *Don Giovanni* frag ment:

> *Il solo Don Giovanni*
> *M'astrinse a mascherarmi*
> *Egli de tanti affani*
> *E l'unica cagion.*
> *Io merito perdon.*
> *Colpevole non son*
> *La colpa è tutta quanta*
> *Di quel femineo sesso*
> *Che l'anima gl'incanta*
> *A gl'incanterà il cor.*
> *O sesso sedutor!*
> *Sorgente di dolor!*
> *Lasciate andar in pace*
> *Un povero innocente*
> *Non sono contumace*
> *Offendervi non so*
> *E ve lo provero*
> *In lui che sie spogliò*
> *Ei prese i panni miei*
> *Per bastonar Masetto*
> *Con Donna Elvira io fei*
> *Il solo mio dover*
> *Fu tale il suo voler*
> *Quel che vi dico e'ver*
> *Merita vostro sdegno*

Il solo Don Giovanni.
Iro a punir l'indegno
Lasciatemi scappar

Lep.: *Incerto,*
Confuso,
Scoperto,
Deluso,
Difendermi non so
Person vi chiederò.

D. Elvira
D. Ott.: *Perdonarti non si può.*
Mas.
Zerl.

Lep.: *Solo da voi dipende*
Il mio fatal destino
Da voi la gracia attende
Il palpitante cor.

D. Elv.: *Devi calar lo spirito*
D. Ott.: *Appeso ad un patibolo*
Mas.: *Vo divorarti l'anima*
Zerl.: *Io vò mangiar la viscave*
a 4) *Infame traditor*
Lep.: *Solo da voi dipende*
Il mio fatal destino
Da voi la gracia attende
Il palpitante cor.

a 4) *Alla forca, alla forca, alla forca*
Lep.: *Che morte, sporca!*
a 4) *In galera, in galera, in galera*

Lep.:	*Rema, bussa, vita sustara!*
a 4)	*Vade a scoppar la piazza*
Lep.:	*Sono di illustre razza*
a 4)	*Dunque la barcha strascinerà*
Lep.:	*Ah no signori per carità*
a 4)	*Che dobbiamo dunque far*
	Del perfido impostar
Lep.:	*Solo da voi dipende*
	Il mio fatal destino
	Da voi la gracia attende
	Il palpitante cor.

CHAPTER TWENTY-EIGHT

ANTI - DA PONTE

D A PONTE was able to maintain himself in his position as long as Joseph II protected him. He wrote a number of further librettos for Italian operas—*Il Talismano* (after Goldoni) for Salieri (September 10, 1788); *Il Pastor fido* (after Guarini) for the same composer (February 11, 1789); *L'Ape Musicale* (February 27, 1789), a *pasticcio* in which twelve composers were represented; then, for Salieri, *La Cifra* (December 11, 1789). Then there was another climax with Mozart's *Cosi fan tutte*. This opera was first performed on January 26, 1790. On April 13 there followed *Nina ossia la Pazza per Amore*, with music by Paisiello and Weigl; on August 13 *La Quakera spiritosa*, with music by Guglielmi. On September 15 *La Caffettiera bizzara*, with music by Weigl, was given, and finally, on March 23, *L'Ape musical riunovato*, another *pasticcio*. Added to this is the cantata *Flora e Minerva*, composed by Weigl, and the oratorio *Davide*, the composer of which is unknown.

Da Ponte became involved in a number of intrigues, the details of which it is very difficult to unravel today, and in the course of time his situation in Vienna became impossible. The main reason was that he championed his mistress, the singer Adriana Ferraresi (to whom he seems to have been absolutely beholden), to such an extent as to earn the disfavor of the Emperor and Empress both for himself and the singer. There was something less than enthusiasm for her at Vienna, yet Da Ponte applied for a six-month renewal of her contract. According to Da Ponte, the Director of Theaters, Count Orsini-Rosenberg, surreptitiously gave the news to Ferraresi's greatest rival, the singer Irene Tomeoni, who on her part wrote fiery and agitated letters to the Empress, letters full of charges against Da Ponte.

"Let these disturbers of peace and quiet be sent to the devil," the Emperor is supposed to have exclaimed vehemently. This, at least, is what Da Ponte says. But Gugitz, in his German edition of Da Ponte's memoirs, reprints a pamphlet entitled "Anti Da Ponte," written by an anonymous but virulent enemy. This represents the matter in a rather different light. According to this story a number of new opera singers had been engaged for the Italian Opera. To deter them from coming—all on behalf of his mistress—Da Ponte is supposed to have sent these singers anonymous letters, giving unfavorable descriptions of conditions in Vienna and especially at the Opera.

Da Ponte knew about the conspiracy on the part of his enemies—most of them, characteristically enough, Italians, his fellow countrymen. He sought an audience with the Emperor and when this was denied, he wrote a bold letter to him which, on top of everything, he had printed and distributed. It is this letter that is the basis for the aforementioned "Anti Da Ponte," criticizing the *Abbé* so bitterly.

In the second part of the pamphlet the "accusers" of Da Ponte are listed, including the "Punch" *(Kasperl)* of the Leopoldstadt Theatre who complains that Da Ponte has invaded his domain. Low comedy had been reserved to the suburban theater, but in his farces, which he called "comic operas," Da Ponte was supposed simply to have plagiarized Viennese low comedy. One had only to look at *Caffettiera bizzara,* in which so much silly stuff occurred! If Da Ponte insisted on further competing with *Kasperl,* the Leopoldstadt Theatre would run a play to be entitled *Kasperl, the Court Poet,* while the *Theater auf der Wieden* would give *The Poetic Fumbler.*

The poet Guarini appears in the pamphlet, complaining that Da Ponte had ruined his work, *Il Pastor fido.* Dittersdorf likewise has nothing good to say about Da Ponte. He had got only a wretched text when he wanted to write an opera for the Italian theater. Dittersdorf also speaks of the efforts of the Italian singers to make his works fail. Give a German the chance, Dittersdorf states, and he can do as well as any Italian. (There is no evidence that Da Ponte ever wrote a libretto for Dittersdorf. Perhaps Dittersdorf rejected him at the start.)

Then Metastasio appears to complain that he has received such unworthy successor. His testimony is offered not so much because Da Ponte had so often expressed himself contemptuously about Metastasio, but because Metastasio is eager to have greater care exercised henceforth in filling the post of court poet.

Beaumarchais is especially furious at Da Ponte who, he claims, has not understood *Figaro,* else he would not have made a changeling out of him. As for how Da Ponte treated *Tarare,* that is something Beaumarchais can never forgive. It was evidence of Da Ponte's low mind and vaulting ambition, that Beaumarchais, the real author, was not even mentioned on the billboards. Da Ponte is charged with having learned from the gypsies how to kidnap strange children, disguising and crippling them.

Martini charges the librettist with having represented himself as the author of the two operas, *Una Cosa rara* and *L'Arbore di Diana,* whereas he, Martini, had brought the plays from Spain and Da Ponte had changed virtually nothing in them. Then Salieri and Mozart appear to complain about the tasteless, clumsy, and disconnected librettos Da Ponte had on several occasions submitted to them. They had had to have recourse to every ounce of their skill in order to present anything harmonious to the public, despite the dry texts. They were firmly resolved never again to set to music anything from the pen of Da Ponte.

In conclusion there is a spokesman for the Vienna public who insists that Da Ponte had been wanting in respect for it, even going so far as to curse the whole German nation when his works were not found acceptable.

As for Da Ponte's defense, it is a farce in which the librettist is presented as a kind of clown.

Da Ponte's destiny in Vienna had come full circle. All his efforts to regain favor remained fruitless. He finally forced an audience with Emperor Leopold, but this too had no effect and he was expelled from the city.

The poet had meanwhile made many attempts to mend his fortunes. These included an effort to enlist Mozart's aid. We reproduce here a letter from Mozart, "to an unkown addressee," dated "Vienna, September, 1791," which undoubtedly is relevant in this connection:

"Dearly esteemed sir: I should like to follow your advice, but how shall I get to it? My head is in a whirl. I have done what was within my power, but the image of the stranger will not vanish before my eyes. I see him forevermore. He pleads with me, he urges me, he impatiently demands the work. I carry on, therefore, for writing it tires me less than repose. In truth I have no cause to tremble. I sense it beyond question. The hour strikes. I am about to die. I have ceased to take pleasure in my skill. How fair life has been! My career began under the most auspicious circumstances. But no one can escape his destiny. No one is his own master. One must become reconciled to what Providence has ordained. And therefore I finish my dirge. I dare not leave it uncompleted. Mozart."

This moving letter was one of Mozart's last. In its reference to "the hour strikes" it seems to allude to "The Magic Flute." It reflects Mozart's fear of death, his fear of the unknown patron who had commissioned the "Requiem." It casts a curious light on Mozart's relationship to Da Ponte, for this letter, among the most touching the composer ever wrote, is addressed to the man who was an outcast from Vienna. No, surely Mozart was not of the anti-Da Ponte faction!

Mozart died two months later. It is noteworthy that Da Ponte does not mention his death in a single line, neither in his memoirs nor in his letters.

CHAPTER TWENTY-NINE

DID DA PONTE RETURN TO THE
JEWISH FAITH?

DA PONTE'S sojourn in Trieste was destined to be of great importance to his further life. He met a girl whom he married, thus taking a step which canon law punished with excommunication. The girl was an English Jewess, Nancy Grahl (Ann Celestine) daughter of a merchant named John Grahl who, together with his son Peter, conducted a business in chemicals and drugs. Father Grahl had been born in Dresden, and his original name was probably Krall (or Kral), a Czech cognomen implying that he may have come from Bohemia.

In a letter of November 16, 1793 to Casanova from the Venetian nobleman Zaguri, who has already been mentioned, we read: "As for Da Ponte, do you know that this Nancy is an English Jewess? A man of my acquaintance, a certain Savadello, was utterly amazed at the marriage. He could scarcely believe his eyes when he saw her married to an *abbé* who was reading mass in the synagogue according to Hebrew rites. I am willing to wager that you don't know the story, because Da Ponte will have kept silent about it. It is possible that Savadello is hoaxing me, but that is hard to believe, for in his story he casually mentions Da Ponte's love affair with Ferraresi!" On March 19 Zaguri again wrote to Casanova: "How on earth could *Abbé* Da Ponte have himself taken for a Jew in Trieste, where he has been living for a long time?"

The question of whether Da Ponte really married in the Jewish faith seems to have preoccupied Casanova deeply. He wrote in the matter to his friend, Baron Pietro Antonio Pittoni, Prefect of Police at Trieste (whom Da Ponte too singles out for praise in his memoirs). Pittoni replied: "Da Ponte married no Jewess. He left Trieste with the so-called daughter of an English merchant named Krahl." (This was written on April 15, 1794.) But Pittoni is wrong. We are probably right in assuming, with Gugitz, that Da Ponte entered only into a common-law marriage with Nancy Grahl, never marrying her in a church ceremony. Perhaps he practiced his pious fraud of recalling his Jewish descent and faith in order to dispel the apprehensions of his mistress rather than to assuage his own conscience.

This would be sufficient to explain why Da Ponte's first biographer, the Catholic priest Bernardi, felt constrained to establish that the poet had rued his error. "The Bishop of New York," he writes, "John McCloskey, head of the congregation where Da Ponte died, was questioned by Rome about the poet's conversion and stated that Lorenzo's last days were marked by evidences of sincere repentance." This would seem to indicate that Da Ponte, after the death of his wife (who was buried December 12, 1831) returned to the bosom of the True Church. A more plausible explanation, so it seems to me, is that Da Ponte did in his marriage use certain rites that accorded with the Anglican faith of his wife, and that Casanova's correspondents interpreted these as being "Jewish." The fact that Nancy herself was of Jewish descent is shown rather clearly by her portrait, which has been preserved. It is quite possible that Da Ponte was never properly married in an ecclesiastical or even legal sense.

CHAPTER THIRTY

DA PONTE VISITS CASANOVA

IN the fall of 1792 we have a glimpse of Da Ponte, traveling from Trieste to Paris. He occupied a carriage with his wife and a servant. He first went to Prague. One may imagine his feelings in passing through the Bohemian capital, five years after the glorious première of *Don Giovanni*. Now his star had paled. He had been abandoned by the world of the theater. He was embarked on an adventurous career that was to take him to the lower depths of life.

His finances were in a poor state and disaster threatened when he lost all his cash near Admont in Styria. He left his Prague address with the Abbot of Admont, who promised to send on the money as soon as it was found. But he waited for it in vain, and not until much later was the purse forwarded to London and thence to the Netherlands. But while in Prague, he was able to witness the tri-

248

umphs of the operas he had written for Mozart. "This sojourn, "Da Ponte says, "afforded me the greatest pleasure in that I was able to hear all three operas I had written for Mozart.

"It is difficult," he continues, "to describe the enthusiasm with which the Bohemians received this fine music. In almost every country these operas met with little admiration when first performed. But the Bohemian people regarded them as heavenly creations. It is a curious thing that the great beauty of the music of this rare and precious genius was discovered by other nations only after many performances, while the Bohemians were aware of it the very first time, understanding it perfectly."

Da Ponte somehow remembered that not far from Prague lived his old friend Casanova, who still owed him several hundred gulden, borrowed long ago. He met Casanova in Oberleutensdorf, where Count Waldstein had his cloth-weaving factory. Da Ponte's young wife was amazed at the wit and temperament of the gallant Venetian—but Lorenzo did not collect his money. Casanova's own exchequer was in even greater straits than Da Ponte's. Escorting the couple to Teplitz on their way to Dresden, he acted as the agent in selling Da Ponte's carriage. And Casanova, who in better times had ridden behind liveried servants in a coach-and-four—Casanova actually pocketed a commision of four ducats! In return he gave Da Ponte three pieces of advice—

to go to London rather than Paris; never to visit the Italian café in London; and never to sign his name to a note. "All my misfortune," Da Ponte complained later, "would have been avoided, had I followed Casanova's counsel."

In Oberleutensdorf near Dux Da Ponte had also met Casanova's patron, Count Waldstein. He was to meet the Count again when that passionate sportsman went to London to purchase horses. Da Ponte now bombarded Casanova with letters pleading for intercession with the Count. But all Casanova did was to give him the cynical advice to exploit his wife's charms. . . .

CHAPTER THIRTY-ONE

CORRESPONDENCE WITH CASANOVA

THE Casanova archives at Hirschberg contain a
large number of letters from Da Ponte to his
friend in Dux. Undoubtedly the meeting between
the two gave new substance to the old relationship.
Even from Dresden, where Da Ponte arrived on
September 21, he wrote to Casanova. His effects had
been stolen on the journey from Teplitz, and en
route to Paris—not far from Speyer—he learned of
the disturbances in Paris and of the imprisonment
of Queen Marie Antoinette. He remembered Casanova's advice not to go there but to pick London
for a sojourn. He quickly changed his plans. The
couple took lodgings with Nancy's sister Louisa
(who was married to a certain Charles Niccolini),
but soon found a home of their own. Da Ponte gave
Casanova his London address as "7, Silver Street,
Golden Square," and later he lived at 16, Sherard
Street, Golden Square.

Da Ponte had scarcely arrived in London when

he began to pay close attention to the Italian theatrical world there. But his statements in his memoirs are not quite correct, for at his arrival it was not William Taylor who was running the Opera (the Drury Lane Theatre in Haymarket), but Michael Kelly and Stefano Storace, as he correctly writes in a letter to Casanova.

Here again we learn more from Da Ponte's correspondence with Casanova than we do from his memoirs. In four letters Da Ponte describes to his friend his failure to find work as a writer for the London theater. The main obstacle was another writer, Carlo Francesco Badini, who pursued him everywhere. For some time Da Ponte was supported by Count Waldstein, to whom he had appealed before, though then without success, through Casanova.

Casanova apparently advised Da Ponte to make his way in London by giving language lessons. This Da Ponte persistently rejected, since it was a profession engaged in by every "lackey, cobbler, and bandit." Unable to get anywhere in London, while his wife was anticipating confinement, Da Ponte resolved to try his luck in Brussels, from where he wrote for the first time on July 18, 1793, though he had been there since July 10. Evidently he tried again to found a theatrical enterprise, but this failed because of intrigues on the part of the singer Nancy Storace. Again he vainly implores Count Waldstein for money, only to turn at last to the Netherlands. He says not a word about the Belgian episode in his memoirs.

Nor does he mention the fact that the post of official theater poet in London had been vacant since 1792, when Antonioli had died, and was actually offered to Da Ponte. We learn this again from his correspondence with Casanova. Da Ponte, however, in an effort to avoid trouble, proposed Badini, a poet and critic, who had resided in London for twenty-five years. When Badini had been appointed, Da Ponte nevertheless announced publication of a magazine, *La Bilancia teatrale,* with which he wanted to intimidate the theater administration to his own advantage. It did not take long for the customary cat-and-dog fight to develop between Bandini and Da Ponte. He tells in his memoirs how he received aid through the composer Pozzi (*Carlo Pozzi,* not *Pietro dal Pozzo,* as falsely stated by Russo in his *Lorenzo Da Ponte,* New York, 1922, and also by Livingston in his English edition of the memoirs). Pozzi introduced him to the famous singer La Mara who asked him to write a play for her at a fee of thirty guineas.

It was with this money that Da Ponte went to the Netherlands. But there too he had a wretched time. Again he appealed to Casanova, this time actually in verse. But the reply started as follows: "When Cicero wrote to his friends, he never spoke of business. . . ." The emergency was not over until Da Ponte received news that the London theater director Taylor had engaged him as a librettist.

CHAPTER THIRTY-TWO

DA PONTE IN LONDON

DA PONTE'S theatrical career in London was by no means strewn with roses. Intrigues and more intrigues gave him no rest. Again it was two primadonnas in whose jealousy Da Ponte was embroiled. The great La Mara had given way to Brigitta Giorgi Banti, a singer who then stood at the zenith of her fame—"one of Europe's most famous singers in the *opera seria*," as Da Ponte put it. Arriving with her at Plymouth from Spain in the spring of 1794 on the same packet boat was Anna Morichelli, who "was no less famous in comic opera." Da Ponte describes the two as human monsters whose only virtue was their fine voice. La Banti (whose biography was published in 1869 by her son, Giuseppe Banti, S.J.) he describes as brazen, dissipated, given to drink, and violent; La Morichelli as cunning and vicious. Scarcely had the two singers arrived in London when they sued for the favor of Taylor, the theater director, who soon found himself in Banti's toils.

Da Ponte had to provide two librettos immediately—one, with Banti as the lead, for the conductor Francesco Bianchi (1752?-1811), who had arrived with the singer; the other, with Morichelli as the lead, for the Spaniard Vincenzo Martini, whom Da Ponte had brought from Russia. Martini is described as a gifted, gracious, and easy-going man. He lived with Da Ponte for a while. Though he was having an affair with Morichelli at the time, he also dallied with a young maid in Da Ponte's house, and when she was expecting a child, Martini told everyone willing to listen that Da Ponte was the father.

This gossip led to a quarrel between Martini and Da Ponte who now rose in Taylor's favor because he had insinuated himself with Banti. Indeed, in time Da Ponte became a fixture at the Italian theater—especially after he had endorsed a note for Taylor. Da Ponte again had occasion to remember Casanova's advice never to sign his name to a note in England. Actually this endorsement seems to have been the turning point in his career. True, at first it gained him great influence. He became Taylor's treasurer, purchasing agent, business representative, paymaster, and all-around favorite. But all this was at the cost of becoming involved in a check-kiting scheme that was to be his undoing.

CHAPTER THIRTY-THREE

JOURNEY TO ITALY AND END OF THE ENGLISH CAREER

IN the year 1798 Da Ponte went to Italy. He wanted to visit his family once more, and he also wanted to look around for good singers. He took along his wife and he describes the touching scene when he was reunited with his father and sisters at Ceneda. But he was able to take but little satisfaction in his stay in Venice (which was then occupied by Austrian troops). On every hand he saw the evidence of incipient moral and material decay in the once-powerful city. Yet a melancholy evening glow seems to have dwelt on this last visit of Da Ponte's to his homeland. It was, so to speak, his farewell to Italy, to his youth, to the ancient culture he was soon to leave behind forever....

Returning to London, he took along the singer Maddalena Allegranti with her husband, and the *castrato* Francesco Damiani. The way led across the

Alps and straight across Germany to Hamburg. As for the second chapter of his sojourn in London, which began in March 1799, it was nothing but a series of misfortunes flowing from his work and devotion for Taylor, the theater director. Da Ponte had grossly ignored Casanova's advice never to sign a note. There was a series of protested checks, prosecutions, and arrests, and in the end Da Ponte had to declare himself insolvent. Taylor was not a man given to gratitude. He not only dismissed Da Ponte —he persecuted him as much as he could.

Jewish and Italian blood flowed in Da Ponte's veins. It was quite natural that he should engage in business affairs. His profession as librettist naturally involved the printing of his librettos, and he himself turned printer. When Taylor had discharged him, he established an Italian bookshop. He even became a publisher, bringing out, among other things, J. B. Casti's *Animali Parlanti*. But the lawsuits in the wake of Da Ponte's notes had begun their course. Hell broke over him, even after he was reinstated in the theater, following Taylor's departure in 1801. Of course Da Ponte misses no opportunity to present himself to posterity in as favorable a light as possible. He ascribes all his misfortunes to the depravity and ingratitude of his fellow man. Will the true circumstances ever be known?

The situation came to such a pass that Da Ponte had to consider leaving London and even Europe.

"About this time [1804]," he writes, "my wife received an invitation from her mother who then lived in America." We are probably safe in assuming that this "invitation" was in some way prompted by Da Ponte's misfortunes in London.

Nancy had had her own fortune for some time, and there can be no doubt that Da Ponte wanted to guard these and perhaps other funds from the grasp of his numerous creditors. Thus the departure of his wife with her four children was set for September 20. Profoundly depressed, Lorenzo took his family to the harbor at Gravesend, where they embarked for Philadelphia, and in equal sadness he returned to London, wher new persecutions awaited him. A meeting of his creditors had been held and no less than twelve warrants were issued against him. That was too much even for this most hunted of all poets. He went to the Alien Office and obtained a passport. On March 5, 1805, he followed wife and children to Philadelphia. . . .

CHAPTER THIRTY-FOUR

DA PONTE'S LITERARY WORK IN LONDON

BEFORE we come to the last chapter in Da Ponte's life, his career in America, let us insert a brief report on his work in London. Scene of his endeavors as a librettist and at times also as a theater manager was the new King's Theatre in Haymarket, which had been opened early in 1791 and became the seat of Italian opera on January 26, 1793 (Löwenberg, *Music Review,* vol. VI). Taylor as already mentioned, was the director, and world-famous stars appeared there, such as the great *castrato* Gasparo Pacchierotti, La Mara (replaced by La Banti, as we have seen). The *castrato* himself had no successor (though it was 1820 when the last *castrato* filled a temporary engagement in London, for the age of the *castrati* was drawing to an end).

The season of 1794 began with Cimarosa's famous opera *Il Matrimonio Segreto,* and surprisingly enough we find in the book the name, not of the real librettist, Bertati—but of Da Ponte! It is well to recall that Da Ponte was charged, not without justification, of having made liberal use, in his own *Don Giovanni,* of Bertati's libretto for Gazzaniga's opera, *Don Giovanni Tenorio ossia Il Convitato di Pietro.* It is doubly amusing to read the passage in his memoirs where he describes a visit to Bertati in Vienna. He calls Bertati a wretched poet and says that he found him writing—copying in turn from a number of books that lay on both sides of his table. . . .

This is scarcely the place to enumerate all the operas that were produced at London in Da Ponte's time. Löwenberg lists some forty of them, and Da Ponte's work thus mirrors an interesting chapter in the history of European opera. Unfortunately, in his memoirs, Da Ponte is excessively preoccupied with himself, his misfortune, and his indictment of others. It would have been most interesting had he said something about Haydn's sojourn in London. The composer, in fact, contributed the duet *Quel cor umano,* sung by the *buffo* Morelli and La Morichelli, to Da Ponte's opera *Il Burbero di Buon Core,* with music by Martini, which was first performed on May 17, 1794.

The life Da Ponte led in London was rather strange. It was the life of a literary man who had fallen into the clutches of usurers and businessmen, of a highly gifted man with ardent emotions and a weak character, a man who, driven by burning ambition, was enmeshed in all the intrigues and dangers of unscrupulous theatrical life.

At every juncture in his life Da Ponte turned to the philosopher of Dux—to Casanova, whose literary remains include many letters from Da Ponte in London. It must have been a shock to Da Ponte when he heard in the summer of 1798 that his friend was no longer among the living. Possibly the news of Casanova's death (which occurred on June 4) did not reach London until the fall, when Da Ponte was already on the way to Italy. It is understandable that he found no occasion to discuss Casanova's death in his memoirs, for about this time he was preoccupied with his Italian adventures. But as we shall see, Da Ponte's life was to remain interlinked with that of Casanova.

CHAPTER THIRTY-FIVE

AMERICA

D A PONTE'S life in America was a matter of
constant decline. It was not as though his intellectual powers had lessened! But his restless temperament, his lack of concentration, his inability to
adapt himself to the background of a realistic business world—all these led him toward ruin—for that
is what the remainder of his life in America was,
apart from a few bright moments which even the
New World vouchsafed him.

Da Ponte was by turns a dry-goods salesman, a
distiller, a book dealer, a teacher of Italian, and an
operatic entrepreneur. He lived in New York and
Philadelphia, and also in the small towns of Eliza-
bethtown and Sunbury, Pennsylvania. He met hun-
dreds of shrewd businessmen, who naturally—as
they had done all over the world—cheated him in
America too. When he did find an honest man or a
benefactor (such as Bishop Clemens Moore in New

York, in whose house he gave his first literary and language courses in 1807, or Dr. Barton, a Sunbury physician), he spoke of him with deep gratitude. But woe, if he was disappointed, as by his pupil Robert Coleman Hall (1792-1844), whom he tutored in classical languages for Princeton University! He read Hall a sermon which, in Livingston's words, was tantamount to blackmail. "Surely," Da Ponte cried, "you could have, without denying yourself anything, offered an octogenarian a pittance so that he might at least rest his weary limbs!"

He had nothing good to say about his own family, which "deceived him and did him only harm." His brother-in-law, Dr. Peter Grahl, for selfish reasons advised him to buy goods on credit in Sunbury, thus causing him to lose his fortune. Da Ponte's sojourn in Pennsylvania, he reports in his memoirs, was another unhappy chapter in his life. Defrauded, repaid with ingratitude by his friends, persecuted by cruel and avaricious creditors, he at last quitted the state and blessed the day, April 26, 1819, when he again beheld Manhattan Island from the Jersey shore of the Hudson. . . .

Da Ponte's years in New York were filled with efforts to introduce or rather promote the Italian language and Italian literature in America. Da Ponte actually became a teacher at Columbia College, and he and his wife for a while ran a boarding school. He boasts of having had a whole number of eminent students.

But just as the rays of the sun cast a glow over the late summer afternoon, Da Ponte was to enjoy once more the privilege of basking in the honor of his *Don Giovanni*.

It seems almost to have been providence that it was Da Ponte who was to introduce the "opera of operas" to America. He tells about the American premiere of the opera in the lively style of his memoirs. In the fall of the year 1825 Manuel Garcia with his troupe had come to New York, opening their engagement with Rossini's *Barber of Seville* at the Park Theatre. Krehbiel tells the story of how Da Ponte and Garcia met and how Lorenzo introduced himself to the singer as the famous librettist. Garcia embraced him and danced about the room like a child, singing the *Finch' han dal vino*.

Da Ponte himself relates how he proposed a performance of *Don Giovanni* to Garcia. There was but one difficulty. There was no Don Ottavio in the troupe. But Da Ponte declared himself willing to pay the expenses of a singer for this role. *Don Giovanni* was a great success, though the press was by no means wholly laudatory. "Garcia [who played Don Giovanni]," wrote the weekly *Albion*, "is not much at home in the simple melodies of Mozart." Nor did Barbieri as Donna Anna meet with warm response. Angrisani as Masetto and young Garcia as Leporello came off rather well. "The only person whose performance can be praised without any exception is Mlle. Garcia." Mlle. Garcia, later called Malibran, played Zerlina. As for the singer whom Da Ponte had contributed to pay the part of Don Ottavio, he was quite inadequate and impossible in the eyes of the critics. The conductor, the French pianist Etienne, is not mentioned with a single word.

There is one little-kown witness who has written about this first American performance of *Don Giovanni*. He is Prince Bernard of Saxe-Weimar, son of Duke Carl August, Goethe's friend. The Prince was in America at the time and visited the Park Theatre. He writes: "I went one evening to the Italian Opera in Park Theatre. This opera was established here last autumn and is an attempt to transplant the exotic fruit to American soil. It does not, however, appear adapted to the taste of the public here; at least the speculation of the Italian theater is not so profitable as was expected. The members of this theater came from the Italian Opera in London. At their head was Signor Garcia, a very good bass, and was directed by a French pianist, M. Etienne. *Don Giovanni* by Mozart was given. It was a great satisfaction to me to see this classic piece so well represented."

The Prince had good taste and good judgment.

If the performance was good, some of the credit must undoubtedly go to Da Ponte who had attached himself to the troupe from the very outset. He had, for example, had *Don Giovanni* translated into English, and Garcia had authorized him to have the book printed at his own expense, for sale on his own account. Delivering a shipment to a shop, he happened to buy a lottery ticket. It brought him luck, for it won $500, and Da Ponte blessed Don Giovanni, the theater, and the lottery.

It was small wonder that the Italian stage should refresh the seventy-six-year old Da Ponte's memory of his youth and his successes, especially those he had scored in Vienna. Now that New York had become aware that the librettist of *Don Giovanni* was within its gates, it is quite likely that he relived the time of his glory and success—the time when he, the friend of the fair Ferraresi, basked in the favor of Emperor Joseph II. Perhaps he remembered Casanova too—Casanova, who had been present at the premiere of his great opera in Prague and whose destiny was peculiarly interwoven with the work. The adventures of his old Venetian compatriot and friend may well have come to his mind.

There can be no doubt that Da Ponte, the bookseller, knew the 1822 issues of the magazine *Urania*. In this periodical, published by Brockhaus in Leipzig, three episodes from Casanova's memoirs were published for the first time. The manuscript of the work had been lost for twenty years—or rather it had been in the possession of Casanova's nephew Carlo Angiolini, from whom Brockhaus acquired it through the mediation of a man named F. Grutzel. Perhaps Da Ponte even saw the first edition of the memoirs, published by Brockhaus in 1822 under the title *From the Memoirs of the Venetian Jacob Casanova de Seingalt* in a German translation by Wilhelm von Schütz. Or he may have seen the first French edition, published in 1826/27, likewise by Brockhaus. It can be no accident that Da Ponte's own memoirs began to appear from the press of John Gray in New York in 1823, one year after the librettist presumably saw the first versions of Casanova's memoirs.

Da Ponte did not write his memoirs in a single sitting. His account of his youth and that of his age materially depart from each other in style and language.

It is my belief that it was Casanova's memoirs that caused Da Ponte to write his own. As his first biographer, Fausto Nicolini, says, it is quite likely that he sought to counter certain attacks upon himself at the same time. As happens so often in life, Da Ponte, who was not quite so chaste in his youth as he liked to pretend in his old age, made a great show of his morality in his memoirs. This is in marked contrast to the memoirs of his dead friend Giacomo, whom he actually makes the target of an attack launched on behalf of chastity. No wonder! Casanova's memoirs were written for men like Prince de Ligne, Count Waldstein, and Count Lamberg. Da Ponte's, on the other hand, were addressed to his New York girl students—he states that seventy-five young lassies read the first version—and to men like his Confessor, Bishop McCloskey, and the trustees of Columbia College. Members of these circles would have been profoundly shocked at Casanova's memoirs, had they ever seen them.

Let us reproduce here a poem that is typical of the "chaste" attitude of the writer of *Don Giovanni* in his old age. I published this poem in facsimile in the New York magazine *Opera News*, after Stefan Zweig had found it in a private house in Ossining near New York. It was meant for the album of a Miss Dard and is superscribed:*Il consiglio d'un vecchio nonagenario:*

> *I primi passi appena*
> *Giovinetta innocente, hai finor mossi*
> *Nel vastissimo campo della vita.*
> *Or che l'età t'invita*
> *A spaziar e internarti in tutti i vari*
> *Sentieri sublunari, i detti ascolta*
> *D'un esperto vegliardo.*
> *Quel che offirà al tuo sguardo,*
> *A tùoi passi, al tuo core*
> *In avvenire il mondo*
> *In aspetto giocondo,*

Sappilo, è un labirinto
D'error, di Mostri, e di perigli cinto.

La terra ha Vulcani,
Il Mar ha tempeste,
Ha l'aere uragani
E fulmini il ciel.
E come i serpenti
Ira l'erbe, ed i fiori
Cosi tra gli accenti
Da'rei seduttori
Si celan ... insiide,
Del labbro crudel.
Del drama terribile
Sii pur' spettatrice:
Osserva, ma guardati
Dal renderti attrice
C'a tanto spettacole
Se brami gioir,
Di tutto dei ridere,
De niente scupir.

One could almost believe that Da Ponte, in his old age, was obsessed by a "seduction complex" when one reads the nonagenarian warning innocent girls of the danger of seduction. To him the prototype of the seducer was, of course, his own Don Giovanni, whom he had so often met in the flesh and in less poetic byways in the figure of Casanova.

And so, even in the final part of his memoirs, Da

Ponte once again reverts to Casanova. He describes an incident in Vienna, when the great adventurer, in order to fatten his slim purse, had proposed a Chinese festival to Emperor Joseph II. But first he had visited Da Ponte to borrow 1,000 Reichsthaler. Da Ponte had refused the request. A few days later he had met Casanova in the Emperor's antechamber, but the Emperor too had declined Casanova's proposal. This caused Casanova to let loose floods of abuse against the sovereign whom Da Ponte so deeply venerated. Da Ponte takes occasion, in his memoirs, to point out "the great gulf between my character and that of Casanova."

It is quite true that Da Ponte was always trying to measure himself and his worth against the "worthlessness" of Casanova. But he never attained his purpose. The differences he emphasizes generally turn out to be in Casanova's favor. Casanova was a scoundrel, but an honest scoundrel in the grand manner. The aged Da Ponte was a poor wretch suing for the favors of little men.

There is a German novel, *Der Amerika-Müde* (The Man Who Grew Tired of America), written by the Viennese author Ferdinand Kürnberger and published in Frankfurt in 1855. The novel is a romantic apotheosis of the journey to America by the poet Nikolaus Lenau who, under the name of Moorfeld, leaves tortured Europe to begin a new life in the United States. But he turns back, revolted by the commercial atmosphere of the New World.

There is a touching scene in this novel, an episode in which the hero, Lenau-Moorfeld, at night on a New York street meets an old man, hungry and cold, wrapped in an old coat. Moorfeld compassionately asks the old man whether the summer nights in America are cold. *"Anchi i giorni,"* comes the reply with a sigh. One thing alone still warms him, he says—his memories of greatness.

Moorfeld treats the old man to a glass of wine, which he empties with a solemn *"Evviva Vienna."* And now the memories well up. The old man reveals to the stranger that he is Da Ponte. Beside himself, Moorfeld cries: "Da Ponte, rival to Casti and Metastasio, languishing on the shores of Manhattan!" He stands before the aged poet as though before a sacred relic, overwhelmed with emotion. The thought of gazing at a countenance that was so dear to Mozart carries him away. Amazement and veneration of the old man hold him spellbound.

It takes some minutes before he is able to regain his composure. Then he addresses the old man with an access of chivalry: *Signor Abbé,* I beg you to accept the tribute of my fervent esteem. Wherever culture is to be found on earth, there each man is in your debt. Deeply moved as I am at the misfortune these hostile shores have apparently brought you, I bless the chance that enables me to seize your hand in this hour. I am overwhelmed with appreciation for what it has done for the world. For *Don Giovanni* is the finest flower of musical art, the sweetest and greatest message of the human heart in modern times. And, by God, it is no mere chance that this wreath of honor in our times flowered principally from your verses."

Da Ponte never met with such fervent homage in America. He lived only on his memories—memories he sought in vain to sell to the Americans. He had to write his own eulogies.

Death took his wife from him in 1832, and henceforth only his correspondence with his friends, especially those in Italy, kept him alive. In the English preface to his poem, *Storia Americana ossia il Lamento* (1835), he declared that he had resolved to return to Italy to die there, but a letter from an American benefactor, enclosing $50, made him change his mind.

So unknown were his name and his significance in America that he decided to publish fifty letters from eminent personages in Europe, "to achieve recognition by the testimony of trustworthy men. They are all dear to me, on account of their content as well as the names of the writers. But for me the name of my kind-hearted American benefactor is the jewel in the collection, because of the juncture

at which his letter was written and because of everything he expresses. One such citizen does honor to
any place. Perhaps New York can boast many of his
kind. I shall leave my ashes to that city to which I
have devoted thirty years of my life. Perhaps those
ashes will then receive even from the ill-meaning
and ungrateful *vano conforto di tardi sospiri?"*

The wretched and demoralized circumstances into which the author of *Don Giovanni* had fallen are
glaringly revealed by the incommensurate gratitude
a gift of $50 could evoke from him! Death was the
only possible relief from such misery. . . . Da Ponte
died on August 17, 1838, at nine o'clock in the
evening, at 91 Spring Street, at the corner of Broad-
way. To the credit of his American friends it must
be said that his funeral was a touching event. It took
place in old St. Patrick's Cathedral on 11th Street
near Second Avenue, on August 20. Da Ponte was
interred in the cathedral cemetery. Allegri's *Mise-
rere* was performed, and the pallbearers were respected New York citizens who had been his friends.

His mortal remains shared the fate of those of
Mozart and Casanova. Da Ponte's grave remained
unmarked and was forgotten by the time use of the
cemetery was discontinued in 1850. In 1913 it was
completely obliterated. No New York monument,
no street perpetuates the memory of Da Ponte. A
few portraits have been preserved, notably one from
the brush of the famous inventor of telegraphy,

Samuel F. B. Morse. It hangs in the Union Club in New York.

The lives of Casanova and Da Ponte span more than a century. Casanova was born in 1725. Da Ponte died in 1838. How many men and women the two came to know! How many changes in the field of culture they saw with their own eyes! When Casanova was born, Pergolesi was still alive. In the *Teatro Grimani* the young adventurer still fiddled for such operas of the old Neapolitan school as those of Alessandro Scarlatti, Anfossi, Jomelli. In his old age Da Ponte defended Rossini and even saw *Der Freischütz* by Weber in New York. In Paris Casanova had still witnessed operas by Campra and Rameau, and at Dux he very probably grew familiar with works by Beethoven. As librarian to Count Waldstein he had charge of a large music library.

On the surface the lives of the two men impinged upon music only outwardly, and it may seem far-fetched to approach them from this aspect. Yet there is a deep fascination in these relationships.

It is the everlasting problem of the deep connection between music and the love of the sexes—a theme that has been treated a thousand times over, from the Pied Piper's tune to the *Kreutzer Sonata,* from simple folksong to *Tristan.* Casanova illuminated it from a very special aspect. Although the hero of the world's most noted adventures in love was not primarily a musician, almost every adventure of his somehow had something to do with the opera and ballet. He and his adventures are the earthly counterpart of *Don Giovanni,* in the creation of which Casanova's own destiny was mystically interwoven. Not merely because the librettist of this opera was his friend—and often so envious an imitator (as Leporello is Don Giovanni's envious admirer)—but because he himself had such a mysterious part in the libretto. For *Don Giovanni* is the story of love's pilgrimage, the calendar of conquests by the erotic genius for whom no woman is too high and none too low, from the aristocratic Donna Anna to the country girl Zerlina. In just this way did Casanova pass through all the stages of love, from the Venetian nun and the charming Henriette to the prostitute in the London bawdyhouse. . . .

Yet it was only the music of Mozart that invested Da Ponte's libretto with the glow of immorality.

A strange trinity: Mozart—Da Ponte—Casanova!

THE END

BIBLIOGRAPHY

Abert: Nicolo Jomelli als Opernkomponist (1908).

D'Ancona: Viaggiatori e avventurieri (1912).

Archenholtz: England und Italien (5 vols., 1787).

Arteaga: Le revoluzioni del teatro musicale Italiano (1785).

Barthold: Die geschichtlichen Persönlichkeiten in Casanova's Memoiren (2 vols., 1846).

Bleakley: Casanova in England (1923).

Burney: The present State of Music in France and Italy (1771).

Burney: The present State of Music in Germany, the Netherlands, etc. (1773).

Capon: Casanova à Paris (1913).

Carletta (Valeri): Casanova a Roma (1899).

Conrad: Giacomo Casanova, Eduard und Elisabeth bei den Megamikren (1922).

Contini: Casanova, Uomo di Teatro (Revista italiana del dramma, 1939).

Correspondance Littéraire (1769 ff.).

Croce: I teatri di Napoli dal secolo XV° al XVIII° (1891).

Curiel: Trieste settecentesca (1922).

Da Ponte: Memorie (4 vols., 1883-27).

Dittersdorf: Lebensbeschreibung (Spazier, 1800).

Dounias: Die Violinkonzerte Giuseppe Tartini's (1935).

Eitner: Biographisch-Bibliographisches Quellenlexikon (1900).

Flögel: Geschichte des Grotesk-Komischen (2 vols., 1914).

Fuerstenau: Zur Geschichte der Musik und des Theaters am Hofe zu Dresden (2 vols., 1861-62).

Galvani: I treatri musicali di Venezia nel secolo XVII° (1878).

Gluck-Jahrbuch: Articles by Einstein and Michel on Gluck.

Grellet: Casanova en Suisse (1819).

[Grimm]: Le petit prophète de Böhmischbroda (1753).

277

Grout: A Short Story of Opera (1947).

Gugitz: Casanova und sein Lebensroman (1921).

Gugitz: Denkwuerdigkeiten des Venezianers Lorenzo da Ponte
(2 vols., 1924).

Gugitz: Casanova und Graf Lamberg (1935).

Haas: Musik des Barocks.

Haas: Gluck und Durazzo im Burgtheater (1925).

Haböck: Die Gesangskunst der Kastraten (1923).

Haböck: Die Kastraten und ihre Gesangskunst (1927).

Hinrichs: Entstehung, Fortgang und Beschaffenheit der Russischen
Jagdmusik (1796).

Ilges: Casanova in Köln (1926).

Jansen: Jean-Jacques Rousseau als Musiker (1884).

Junk: Handbuch des Tanzes (1930).

Keyssler: Neueste Reisen durch Deutschland, Böhmen, Ungarn, die
Schweiz, Italien und Lothringen (1751).

Khol und Pick: Giacomo Casanova, Briefwechsel mit J. F. Opitz
(1922).

Kretzschmar: Geschichte der Oper (1919).

Lazzeri: La vita e l'opera letteraria di Raniero Calzabigi (1907).

Ligne, Prince de: Oeuvres posthumes (6 vols., 1817).

Erinnerungen und Briefe (Klarwill, 1920).

Annales (1920, 1921).

Livingston: Memoirs of Lorenzo da Ponte (1929).

Lorme: Carlo Goldoni, Mein Leben und mein Theater (1923).

Löwenberg: Lorenzo da Ponte in London, Music Review IV.

Marcello: Das Theater nach der Mode (Einstein).

Marchesan: Della vita e delle opere di Lorenzo da Ponte (1900).

Maynial: Casanova et son temps (1910).

Molmenti: Carteggi Casanoviani (2 vols., 1917-1919).

Molmenti: Le lettere di Casanova (1916-1918).

Molmenti: La Grandezza di Venezia (1892).

Moritz: Reisen eines Deutschen in Italien (3 vols., 1792-93).

Mueller, Erich: Angelo und Pietro Mingotti (1917).

Musatti: Due teatri "Goldoni" a Venezia (Nuovo Archivio Veneto
XXIII).

Nettl: Casanova and Music (Musical Quarterly, 1929).

Nettl: Mozart in Böhmen (1938).

BIBLIOGRAPHY

Nettl: Casanova and the Dance (1945).

Nettl: The Story of Dance Music (1947).

Nettl: Musik und Tanz bei Casanova (1924).

Nettl: Don Giovanni in New York, Opera News, IX, 5.

Pollio: Bibliographie des oeuvres de Casanova (1926).

Pollio et Vèze: Pages Casanoviennes (8 vols., 1925-26).

Ravà und Gugitz: Giacomo Casanovas Briefwechsel (1913).

Ravà und Gugitz: Frauenbriefe an Casanova (1912).

Ricci: Burney, Casanova e Farinelli in Bologna (1890).

Ricci: I teatri di Bologna nel secoli XVII e XVIII (1888).

Rolland: Histoire de l'Opéra en France avant Lully et Scarlatti (1931).

Rousseau: Confessions (1781-1788).

Rousseau: Dictionnaire de Musique (1768).

Rousseau: Lettre sur la Musique Française (1753).

Rousseau: Les consolations des misères de ma vie (1781).

Russo: Lorenzo da Ponte, Poet and Adventurer (1922).

Saccchi: Vita del Cavaliere Don Carlo Broschi detto Farinelli (1784).

Samaran: Casanova (1904).

Schillmann: Geschichte und Kultur Veneziens (1933).

Schmidt-Pauli: Der andere Casanova (1930).

Schueneman: Geschichte des Dirigierens (1913).

Sittard: Zur Geschichte der Musik und des Theaters am Wuerttem-bergischen Hofe (2 vols., 1890-91).

Terry: J. Ch. Bach (1929).

Teuber: Geschichte des Prager Theaters (2 vols., 1883).

Thuerheim: Karl Josef Fuerst de Ligne (1877).

Wiel: I teatri musicali di Venezia nel settecento (Nuovo Archivio Veneto, 1891).

279

INDEX

INDEX